BASKETBALL
The Modern Way

By

J. G.

GARSTANG

STERLING PUBLISHING CO., Inc.   NEW YORK

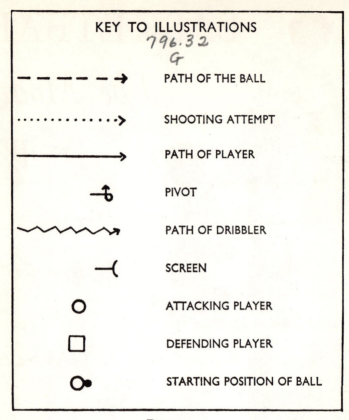

KEY TO ILLUSTRATIONS

796.32
G

PATH OF THE BALL

SHOOTING ATTEMPT

PATH OF PLAYER

PIVOT

PATH OF DRIBBLER

SCREEN

ATTACKING PLAYER

DEFENDING PLAYER

STARTING POSITION OF BALL

DIAGRAM I

Revised Edition Copyright © 1967

© 1961 J. G. Garstang

First published in the United States of America in 1962 by
Sterling Publishing Co., Inc.
419 Park Avenue South, New York, N.Y. 10016

Contents

947

BASKETBALL COURT DIAGRAM

IF COURT IS LESS THAN 74 FEET LONG IT SHOULD BE DIVIDED BY TWO LINES, EACH PARALLEL TO AND 40 FEET FROM THE FARTHER END LINE.

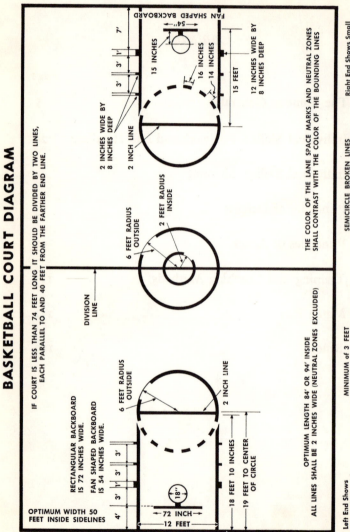

THE COLOR OF THE LANE SPACE MARKS AND NEUTRAL ZONES SHALL CONTRAST WITH THE COLOR OF THE BOUNDING LINES

OPTIMUM LENGTH 84' OR 94' INSIDE
ALL LINES SHALL BE 2 INCHES WIDE (NEUTRAL ZONES EXCLUDED)

Left End Shows
Large Backboard
for College Games.

MINIMUM of 3 FEET
Preferably 10 feet of unobstructed space outside. If impossible to provide 3 feet, a narrow broken 1" line should be marked inside the court parallel with and 3 feet inside the boundary.

SEMICIRCLE BROKEN LINES
For the broken line semicircle in the free throw lane, it is recommended there be 8 marks 16 inches long and 7 spaces 14 inches long.

Right End Shows Small
Backboard for High School and Y.M.C.A. Games.

1   *The Game in General*

Origin of Basketball

BASKETBALL IS probably the only team game that has been invented rather than evolved, and although the standard of play has progressed enormously since its early beginnings the present day game differs little in principle from the one that is reputed to have had its debut in 1891. It was in this year that a Dr. James Naismith of Springfield College, Massachusetts, is credited with inventing the game we now know as basketball. By all accounts it would appear that he had been instructed by his College principal to devise a suitable activity that could be played indoors and which would help the students of the College to remain fully active in the winter when football and baseball were not possible. By virtue of the conditions of space and surface imposed by a gymnasium Dr. Naismith apparently decided to introduce a ball game that would exclude rough play and put emphasis upon skill; hence the goals were put out of reach of the players, personal contact was ruled out and running with the ball was illegal. So when the students at Springfield College played this game in which they attempted to score points by throwing a soccer ball into a suspended peach basket, according to a dozen or so rules that Dr. Naismith had drawn up, basketball was born.

As the game has developed, and the original rules altered and expanded, its character has remained essentially the same. Indeed, many of the amendments have been concerned solely with preserving Dr. Naismith's original concept of maximum activity allied to skill, and it is this feature of the game that gives it its immense appeal to both players and spectators. Even now, when the game has reached a degree of stability, there is support for the introduction of measures that would reduce still further the advantages that can be gained by the very tall player purely because of his physical height. Previous alterations to the rules have progressively increased the dimensions of the free throw lane in an effort to prevent the tall player from dominating the game as a goal-hanger. At one time he could position himself with impunity a mere three feet from the basket and on receiving the ball could, because of his superior height, drop it immediately through the ring with the minimum of movement. Under the present rules he is considerably restricted in this respect for the distance has now tripled. Moreover, the National Basketball Committee, the official rule-making body of the National Collegiate Athletic Association and the National Federation of State High School Athletic Associations, has recently barred dunking, a shot utilized mostly by tall players. Dunking is dropping the ball into the basket while holding it above the rim or stuffing it through, and the penalty is loss of possession. The purpose of this new rule is to equalize the offense and defense and to give each team similar privileges under the basket. From the beginning of basketball, the ball was to be thrown, not pushed, through the hoop.

From the tentative start in 1891, the game grew quickly in popularity throughout America due initially to the activities of the Y.M.C.A., for Springfield College was a training center of this organization. Inevitably the game spread elsewhere because of the Y.M.C.A.'s international influence but it was not until 1932 that the International Basketball Federation (F.I.B.A.) was set up as the controlling body of the sport. This association, which now has some 80 member countries, is concerned primarily with establishing and standardizing the rules of play, sponsoring the principal tournaments of international competition and safe-guarding the best interests of the game in general.

The International Scene

Basketball was first featured in the Olympic Games as far back as 1904 but it was not until the Games were held at Berlin in 1936 that it was included officially as one of the competing sports and it has been firmly established in the Olympic program ever since (sure confirmation that it is recognized as a major sport). After each Olympic Games the F.I.B.A. delegates normally meet to discuss probable changes in the rules with a view to improving the game on the evidence of the tournament just completed and the lessons learned during the preceding four years of competition. However, it is expected that the rules adopted after the 1960 Olympic Games in Rome will be allowed to stand for 8 years, instead of the customary 4 years, before making any changes.

The Olympic Games can be regarded as the supreme testing ground of relative prowess in the various sports and it is significant to note that every Olympic basketball tournament has been won by a team representing the United States. Without doubt this country has been responsible for not only the invention of the game itself but also for its subsequent development to the present high standard. Basketball has become a leading spectator and participant sport in the United States and it is claimed that the American players have made a fine art of the game's techniques and the American coaches a science of its tactics. It is certainly true to say that the American players and coaches—and spectators—are the most knowledgeable and experienced and their enthusiasm for the game has helped to bring it to the forefront of the international sporting scene.

With the resumption of the Olympic Games in 1948, and with the increased amount of international competition and interchange of players and coaches, the rest of the world has been able to learn from the Americans and make up a great deal of the leeway. We now find that world standards are reaching a more uniform level, though most countries still look to America for guidance on trends in techniques and tactics. It would seem that

America's closest rivals are some of the South American countries, notably the Argentine and Brazil, for these countries have more than made their presence felt in the World Championships even to the extent of ousting the United States from first place. However, this major competition, which was inaugurated in 1950, is still in its infancy and the results of the tournaments so far held do not give as accurate a guide to world rankings as those of the Olympic Games.

The progress of the game in Europe during the past few years has been remarkable and it is now enjoying unprecedented popularity nearly everywhere. The standard of play varies greatly from one country to another but there is little doubt that the time is not far distant when many will be able to compete on level terms with the best in the world. Even now such countries as Russia and Czechoslavakia are rapidly approaching the standard of the leaders and are far from outclassed in their company. A contributory factor to the growth of the game in Europe that cannot be discounted is the tremendous impact made by those acclaimed Ambassadors of Basketball, the Harlem Globetrotters, who since the end of the second world war have made regular appearances on both sides of the Atlantic giving exhilarating exhibitions of their phenomenal skill. While it must be admitted that these players are first and foremost professional entertainers, it cannot be denied that they are remarkable exponents of basketball skill and as a result have done untold service in stimulating interest in the game. Their performances have been witnessed—and enjoyed—by countless millions of people each year and though the purists may decry their antics at the very least the Harlem Globetrotters have made the general public aware of the game of basketball.

Equipment

ALTHOUGH THE rules of basketball, and to some extent the game itself, understandably appear complex to the uninitiated the actual material requirements are comparatively simple. All that is needed is a playing area, goals and a ball.

The regulation size for the playing area, or court as it is more commonly termed, is a rectangle 84 feet long by 50 feet wide with variations of up to 10 feet in length, and this court should have markings as laid down in the rules. The ideal measurements for basketball courts can be found in the official rules on page 139.

A reduced playing area does affect adversely the quality of the play possible and teams that are accustomed to such conditions are handicapped when they do come to play on a regulation size court. Small courts also call for the exercise of greater care on the part of both players and officials because personal contact, and therefore injury, is more likely to occur as the players are moving about at speed in a confined space. This is especially true when attempts are made to utilize to the utmost the limited area available and there is little or no margin between the boundary lines and the walls.

The surface of a basketball court is normally of wood, asphalt or other hard and permanent composition; therefore little or no maintenance need be carried out other than an occasional repainting of the floor markings. What is of even more significance is the fact that basketball courts can be multilateral in use, providing facilities for a wide range of activities if so desired, ranging from the normal gymnasium pursuits to such extremes as dancing and roller skating. These are economic factors that provide a strong argument in favor of the provision of more basketball courts.

Basketball courts need not be restricted only to indoor establishments for it is a game that can be played equally well out-of-doors.

The only fixtures on any basketball court, whether indoors or outdoors, are the goals and these consist of 18-inch diameter metal rings rigidly attached to rectangular backboards at a height of 10 feet from the ground. These backboards, usually made of hardwood or transparent material, 6 feet by 4 feet, should also be rigid so that the rings are in fact a constant target and not subject to any form of deviation. According to the rules, the backboards should overhang the court by four feet but on very small courts this brings the two goals too close together. In these circumstances it is recommended most strongly that on no account should backboards be affixed flush to the walls of the gymnasium for in addition to affecting certain shooting techniques by giving the players no room to drive under the basket (and this can prove a permanent handicap if bad habits are formed) it also presents a very real physical hazard to the players as it means there is no margin at all between the end line and the wall. A reasonable compromise is to have the boards projecting two feet into the court. To complete the goals, the backboards should have markings in the form of a border around the edges and a rectangle, 2 feet by 18 inches, with the lower side centered behind the ring. The ring itself should have a tapered net attached so that the ball is checked momentarily as it passes through, enabling the players and officials to determine whether or not a basket has been scored.

On outside courts in particular, a portable type of goal is frequently used and it is not uncommon for this version to be fitted with a smaller backboard in order to reduce the problem of wind resistance and the difficulties of construction presented by the weight of a full size backboard. As with smaller courts, a modification of this nature is to be preferred to no basketball at all. For the same reason that it is dangerous to affix backboards flush to the wall, it is dangerous to have supports or obstructions immediately below these backboards; therefore they, too, should have a clear overhang of at least 2 feet into the court.

The final item of compulsory equipment is, of course, the ball. Originally the ball used was a common soccer ball but now the official ball is somewhat larger and heavier, its circumference being $29\frac{1}{2}$ to 30 inches and its weight being 20 to 22 ounces. Inflated to the correct pressure a basketball should bounce to a height somewhere between 49 inches and 54 inches when dropped from a height of 6 feet from the floor. This is a stipulation invariably overlooked, even by prominent teams, yet it is one that can substantially affect the rebounding qualities of the ball.

The type of ball now in general use is of molded rubber, usually covered with a skin of leather, rubber or synthetic material, and is inflated by means of a needle valve. Though rather an expensive item this type of ball is infinitely superior in life and performance to its forerunner the lace-up pattern, and any team desirous of playing good basketball is urged to use only top quality, approved basketballs. Admittedly the game can be played with an inferior type of ball but this will impede progress and in many instances even result in causing faulty techniques. For example, when dribbling with a poor quality ball that does not have a true bounce the player cannot anticipate accurately its response at any given moment; therefore he is forced to focus his attention on the ball instead of the situations around him. With a perfect ball, the competent dribbler can proceed without looking at it and so is able to respond immediately to any opportunity that may present itself.

Apart from the items used by the various officials to conduct the game, the remaining equipment needed to play basketball is the player's personal clothing. Here the greatest attention must be given to choice of footwear. In basketball, the player is continually moving quickly about the court, constantly changing direction, varying his speed, turning, jumping, starting and stopping rapidly. These are all actions that throw severe demands upon the feet and are techniques that cannot be executed efficiently, or without causing considerable discomfort if not actual damage, in other than the appropriate footwear. It is wrong to attempt to play competitive basketball in normal gymnasium sneakers and every player is advised to invest early in his playing career in a pair of sneakers specially designed for basketball. It is often stated, and not without justification, that a basketball player is no better than his feet; certainly he soon becomes a liability to the team if he has not given his feet due consideration. In addition to wearing the correct outer footwear the player should always wear comfortable, well-fitting socks that absorb moisture and allow the feet to breathe.   A further precaution against injury and discomfort that is practiced by many players is the application of talcum powder before and after play.

The minimum personal equipment is completed by shirt and shorts and these are designed to permit the maximum freedom of movement. Invariably these are attractive and colorful in appearance and while a smart uniform cannot influence technical ability it can certainly help to inculcate a healthy team spirit. Each player must carry a number on both the back and front of his shirt, normally any number from 4 to 15, so that during play everyone on court can be immediately identified by the controlling officials and the scorer. The scorer has to keep a record not only of each individual player's score but also of all the fouls and free throws that are awarded during the course of the game. In view of the speed of basketball and the high rate of scoring his task would be well nigh impossible if every player were not clearly and individually marked in this way.

Although not part of the regulation attire it is essential that players should equip themselves with track suits or other form of warm top clothing that can be quickly slipped on or off. During the course of a game a player may be called upon to enter or leave the court at short notice and this top clothing enables him to keep warmed up while on the bench, especially when he has just played an energetic period, thus lessening the chance of injury should he return to the game. There is no limit to the number of times a player may be substituted into the game but there is a limit to the amount of time that can be consumed in carrying out a substitution, and as this is a mere 20 seconds it is understandable that players should only wear top clothing that can be taken off easily! A player struggling with an awkward garment may cost his team dearly.

The Game

Basketball is a game that requires speed, skill and stamina and by the same token it is a game that helps to develop these attributes at no matter what level it is played. Unlike most sports it does not put strength, either specialized or general, at a premium; and as personal contact is excluded serious physical injuries are far less prevalent than in other team games. Instead of strength the emphasis is upon skill, yet at the same time it is a game that virtually anyone can learn to play and enjoy, and as such is an ideal sport for inclusion in the program of schools, colleges, youth clubs, and other organizations where people pursue recreational activities. It is a team game in the true sense of the phrase and individual merit can only be assessed in terms of the contribution to the team effort. Unfortunately, the tall player still has a definite advantage over his smaller counterpart, but it cannot be stressed too forcibly that height alone is not the criterion of success. Far more important are physical and mental alertness, good co-ordination and technical ability, and a genuine enthusiasm for the game. If these assets are combined with superior physical height we have the ideal player.

According to the official rules, basketball is a game that is played by two teams of five players each with the object of throwing the ball into the opponents' basket and at the same time preventing the other team from securing the ball or scoring. In the course of the game the ball may be passed, thrown, batted, rolled or dribbled in any direction subject to certain restrictions. How little does this formal definition convey of the skills and techniques that are involved or of the exhilarating play that can be produced!

Basketball is reputed to be the fastest team game on foot. This conclusion is not based on the speed of the players themselves, nor upon the speed of the ball as it travels about the court, but rather upon the speed of incident that occurs in the game and this is borne out by present day scoring rates where one goal every 30 seconds is not unduly exceptional. In no other game do attack and defense switch so rapidly from one team to the other. This aspect of the game has been heightened by many of the rule changes in recent years, measures having been introduced to speed up the play to an even greater degree. Probably the alteration that had most effect in this direction was the abolition of the center jump that used to take place after the scoring of every basket. Now, play continues without pause because the defending team automatically gains possession immediately after the basket is scored.

The time factor is featured prominently throughout the rules of play, many of which are concerned exclusively with imposing time limits that have been responsible for dictating the pattern that the game has taken over the years. Accurate timing is so important that competitive basketball requires an official who is occupied solely with timekeeping and his duties are no less significant to the game than those of the other officials. During the course of the game he is constantly stopping and starting the game clock, in accordance with the rules, to ensure that there is a full 40 minutes and no more of actual play. He must also keep a careful check for the many time violations that can be committed by a team or individual player. One of the latest amendments is the 24-second rule in professional ball which has been introduced to prevent teams from employing time-wasting tactics. In the past, particularly with professional teams, freezing the ball was a legitimate stratagem frequently employed in the closing minutes of a game if a team led by a narrow margin. By this ruse, a team of expert ball handlers could pass the ball among themselves for minutes on end without the slightest intention of attempting a shot at the basket. The sole object of freezing the ball was to deny the opponents the opportunity of gaining possession and in this way a team could hang on to its lead until the final whistle was blown. Such tactics make for a poor spectacle and are not in the best interests of the game, especially as the more unscrupulous players would adopt these tactics at almost any stage in the game where a lead had been established. With the introduction of the 24-second rule a team must now make a shooting attempt at the basket within 24-seconds of gaining possession; if it outruns this time, play is stopped and possession given to the opponents.

On account of the scientific approach to the problems of attack and defense there has been a tendency for teams to lose sight of the fact that basketball is primarily a game of fundamental skills. It is quite useless for players of limited experience and ability to try and reproduce involved set plays that have been devised and successfully performed in match play by experts. Basketball is a game that can only be worked out in theory if there is sufficient skill and knowledge to back up the theories.

There has also been a tendency to interpret basketball play using known experiences, notably those gained from playing football. This has resulted in a failure to appreciate the importance of possession in a game that is played in a relatively confined space and which protects the ball handler. A fumbled pass, a careless dribble, an attempt at the basket with little hope of success may mean four points have been thrown away—the two points that were possible before possession was lost and the two points the opponents can achieve because they have gained possession! It should be impressed upon players that only the team in control of the ball can score; therefore possession should not be surrendered lightly. In effect this philosophy stresses the need for mastery of the fundamental skills before all else, for the team that is 100 per cent in this department will never forfeit possession of the ball until it makes a shooting attempt at the basket—and then only if it has at least a fifty-fifty chance of succeeding.

Another common result of relating basketball to football is a failure to realize that all players take a full part in both attack and defense. Unlike football, at no time in the game can a player assume he has completed his job and take a breather while the attack, or defense, get on with their phase of the play. As long as he is on court he is directly concerned with the play regardless of the phase in progress. The only means the basketball player has of taking an extended breather, other than during legal stoppages, is for him to be substituted by another player. The matter of substitution has always been alien to the amateur athlete but in basketball it is an integral part of the game, specifically provided for by rules, and if used wisely is an asset to the game. With the high level of physical exertion that is called for in competitive basketball five players could hardly be expected to maintain all-out effort for the full forty minutes. Moreover, with a team of only five players the balance of the game would be destroyed completely should one or more be forced to leave the court due to injuries or accumulation of five fouls and the team denied a replacement. By having substitutes the standard and tempo of the game can be preserved and a greater number of people can take part. A team may in fact consist of up to 12 players, though this privilege is normally only used to the full in tournaments and competitions when the team may be called upon to play more than once, and they can be substituted on and off the court any number of times. As substitution only takes place when the clock is stopped it does not involve any waste of time or detract from the continuity of the play; therefore antagonism to this feature of the game is scarcely justified.

Problems for the Beginner

Mastery of the fundamentals is the basis for success; it is equally true that players can only play the game effectively if they are fully conversant with all the rules and understand their interpretation. This does not infer that the intending player must wait until these requirements have been fulfilled before starting to play the game. On the contrary, the acquisition of the numerous techniques and technicalities should be attained through a gradual process of learning and practice combined with actual playing experience.

A major failing with the beginner at basketball, apart from considerations connected with the rules, is a lack of shooting ability. Most people, particularly those who are inclined towards playing any type of ball game, can usually manage to throw and catch the ball with a moderate degree of success but shooting at a target 10 feet above the ground is a different matter. With very young people it may even amount to a physical impossibility. Therefore, as basketball cannot be played seriously until a reasonable standard of shooting has been reached, it is recommended that the beginner play some simple team passing games incorporating the main principles of basketball play, notably no personal contact and no running with the ball. With regard to the first condition it should be impressed upon beginners that they must not try to take the ball away from an opponent as this is the greatest single cause of contact. With regard to the second condition, they should be made to pass the ball from the point at which it was received. Initially it is advisable to allow, say, three steps in which to receive and pass the ball as complete beginners have not sufficient control to come to an immediate standstill, but this should be gradually reduced to the legal one step. Passing games played in this way form an ideal introduction to basketball for beginners and by the time they are able to cope with the mechanics of shooting they will have improved their general handling techniques, adapted themselves to the essentials of basketball play, and be ready to embark upon the game proper. Needless to say, it is not an immediate step from these introductory games to a full-scale interpretation of basketball. Instead, a simplified version should be played in which rules, techniques and tactics are all kept to the minimum and gradually increased as progress is made or a particular need shown.

In actual fact beginners can do far worse than to play their simplified version of the game according to the rules of Dr. Naismith! The fundamental difference between the game played to these rules and basketball proper is the omission of legal dribbling, but as this is one of the principal reasons for lack of control with beginners it is in their interests to exclude it completely in the early stages. When it is eventually introduced, indiscriminate dribbling must be discouraged at all costs for it slows up the game. It is sometimes difficult to persuade beginners not to dribble the ball each time they receive it because, naturally, they derive considerable pleasure from making repeated contact with the ball. The complete omission of dribbling in the early stages will help to produce a more intelligent approach to this fundamental in future play.

A further limitation that is recommended in early play is with regard to passing and shooting. It is far better for the beginner to concentrate on a few basic methods until really proficient at them than to try and cope with all the different variations. To this end it is suggested that the two-handed chest and bounce passes, together with one- and two-handed set shots, should be the only techniques allowed in these early games.

In the matter of tactics at this formative stage it would seem that the best results are obtained if just a few salient points of policy are introduced. If too many recommendations are thrust upon the beginner the issue will become confused and he will gain little benefit. Defensive measures should be based on straightforward man-to-man principles, each player being responsible for one person only. Players cannot be expected to develop systems of defense until simple man-to-man has become second nature to them. With regard to attack, the emphasis should be upon retaining possession of the ball until a reasonable opportunity for a shot presents itself. (On no account should the 24-second rule be introduced to beginners or they will indulge in careless shooting and play will quickly deteriorate.) The following eight tactical points are sufficient to guide the beginner in his early play.

When your team is in possession:

Use only short, direct passes.

Pass the ball to a player who is unguarded.

After passing the ball, follow it up or move into an open space.

Do not shoot if there is someone better placed.

Try to get away from your opponent so that you are free to receive a pass.

When the opponents are in possession:

Keep between your man and the basket at all times.

Only guard your man closely when he is within shooting range.

Try to see the ball and your man at the same time.

Later, as their game develops, players may find they have to adapt or even reverse these principles in order to meet particular circumstances. However, this simple code will help the beginner to develop his game along the right lines.

Through the medium of simple passing games and a simplified version of basketball the beginner can be initiated into match play and be given a basis on which the full game can be gradually built.

2 *Individual Skills (1)*
Footwork and Ball Handling

THE GOOD player, and indeed the good team, is one that is sound in fundamentals. If the first-rate performance of these is automatic, concentration can be given entirely to the situations of attack and defense and the strategies of the game as a whole. There is no short cut to proficiency in these skills; the individual and the team must learn each one correctly and then perfect it through repeated practice, not just in specific training sessions but in every spare moment possible. Actual match play is not sufficient on its own account to promote the degree of efficiency that make either a successful player or a successful team. In a 40-minute full-scale game it is conceivable that a player may make only half a dozen or less shots at the basket. If this is to represent his sole method of accumulating technical experience he will never become a competent shooter. However, if this same player devotes, say, 10 minutes of every practice session to perfecting his shooting technique he could, if desired, make 100 or more shots at the basket in this time and so stand infinitely more chance of becoming an expert shooter. The same analogy applies to all the fundamentals. It is erroneous to think that the many techniques of basketball skill can be learned merely by playing the game.

FOOTWORK

Good footwork is a vital fundamental of basketball. In the first instance the use of the feet must comply with certain regulations (see the rules) when the player is actually handling the ball, otherwise a technical violation results. Hence, for this reason alone, it follows that every player must give consideration to footwork if he is not to be a recurring liability to his team. Any player who commits a technical violation in the use of the feet while playing the ball automatically deprives his team of possession and gives the initiative to the opponents. Secondly, good footwork can be of tremendous influence in helping a player to outmanoeuvre and outwit the opponents both in attack and defense. A fraction of a second can make or break an opening in basketball; therefore the player with the better footwork will gain the advantage.

Stopping and Starting

The part played by good stopping and starting cannot be overestimated and the sooner beginners accomplish these fundamentals the sooner will they be on their way to becoming basketball players. At all times the ability to stop quickly, with the minimum of warning, is essential for creating or combating the surprise openings upon which the game revolves. When actually taking possession of the ball while he is in motion, a player is limited to two beats of the feet upon the floor in which to come to a standstill no matter how fast he may be travelling.

In coming to a sudden standstill the fast-moving player will lose his balance, thereby losing the intended advantage, if he does not keep his body weight well to the rear. This can only be effected by the player bending quickly at the knees, keeping the back upright, and pushing the feet hard into the floor in front of the body as the stop is made. Beginners can learn this technique by running slowly up and down the court and then quickly sinking into the floor on a given signal to come to a standstill with one foot in front of the other to the count of two. As soon as the stop has been made the legs should be straightened to bring the body into a normal stance. The tempo of this practice can be stepped up gradually until a two-beat stop can be controlled even at full speed.

Beginners will find this hard work upon the feet—especially if they do not have good quality footwear—but should experience no difficulty in recognizing the two-beat rhythm as the feet <u>put on the brakes</u>. This is the method normally employed in coming to a legal standstill with the ball, two beats being allowed from the moment the player has collected the ball, and is called the Stride Stop. Having taken this permitted stride any further pace will constitute <u>travelling</u>, which is a violation of the rules, until such time as he gets rid of the ball. An alternative method of stopping favored by some players is the Jump Stop. In this method the two-beat action consists of a take-off from one foot and then a simultaneous landing on both feet, usually side by side about hip width apart. The Jump Stop is not recommended for beginners as it is more difficult to employ and there is an almost unavoidable tendency for the inexperienced player to announce his intentions well in advance by exaggerating the jump. With experienced players this method can sometimes be used to advantage as it gives greater license in the use of the Pivot (a technique which is described later).

Fast starting is mostly a matter of natural ability but the correct technique can be developed. As with stopping, fast starting can be instrumental in securing the advantage necessary for a scoring opportunity or for countering an opponent's intentions and players should try to make the most of whatever speed they possess. Once again it hinges upon deployment of body weight and the fastest start is obtained by quickly lowering the center of gravity as the drive is made with the feet.

Pivoting

Many successful plays emanate from the use of the Pivot yet for some unaccountable reason it is generally used all too sparingly by players below professional level. The pivot is the ball handler's protection against losing the ball; it is his means of turning a negative situation into a potentially dangerous one. The rules of basketball forbid a player to move from one point on the court to another while holding the ball but do give him the right to pivot with it, a pivot being defined as one or more steps in any direction with the same foot while the other foot retains the same point of contact with the floor. There are limitations governing the choice of pivot foot (*i.e.*, the one that remains stationary) and these depend upon what has immediately preceded the pivot. If a player receives the ball while standing still he may use either foot as the pivot foot, but if he wishes to pivot after coming to a two-beat stop with the ball he may only pivot on the rear foot, assuming he has used the customary

DIAGRAM 2

Stride Stop. However, those players who use the Jump Stop or are capable of coming to a standstill on the first count of the permitted two beats, retain the privilege of pivoting on either foot. The pivot is usually made when confronted by a close guarding opponent in order to protect the ball, to open up a different lane of passing, or to elude the guard prior to taking a shot or commencing a dribble. The pivot is an invaluable technique that should become an instinctive part of every player's repertoire (Diagram 2).

To execute a good pivot the player should bend the knees slightly and lean the head and shoulders into the turn so that the new position is reached in the quickest possible time. On no account must there be any lifting or sliding of the pivot foot as this constitutes a violation; beginners should try to keep the ball of the pivot foot rather than the toe in contact with the floor.

When teaching the pivot the coach should first of all let his players practice it while standing still so that he can correct any faults before drilling them in the use of the pivot after coming to a standstill. Moreover, he should not introduce a ball into the drills until satisfied that the technique of pivoting has been mastered.

Change of Direction

A sudden change of direction while running can be as effective as the previous techniques in creating openings, eluding guards or keeping up with attacking opponents. A change of direction is best achieved by lowering the weight slightly and stabbing one foot out to the side of the general line of direction in order to thrust away vigorously along a different line. With the speed of incident that is prevalent in basketball the advantage that can be gained by the judicious use of this technique will become increasingly apparent to the players.

A more severe change of direction can be obtained by incorporating the pivot action already described. Instead of thrusting to one side and driving along a different line the player executes a quick stop, immediately pivots and breaks away along the new direction in one continuous sequence.

When learning change of direction it can be practiced quite simply, players moving about the court and then cutting along a different line on a given signal until they become accustomed to the technique.

PASSING

With possession being such a dominant factor in basketball the importance of good passing technique need hardly be stressed. While the object of the game is to get the ball into the basket, shooting ability will be to little avail if a team repeatedly loses possession of the ball due to poor passing. Skill in passing and catching should take precedence over all other ball handling fundamentals.

There are many accepted types of passes in basketball, many of which are designed to meet a specific need. There is no place in basketball for the fancy pass. Every pass made in the game should fulfil the requirement that all wasted movement has been eliminated. A complicated behind-the-back pass has no justification if the same result can be achieved by a more ortho-dox method. Passes of this nature are more likely to go astray and may confuse teammates as much as the opponents! So-called fancy passes are the prerogative of such teams as the Harlem Globetrotters who profess to be entertainers; even so, it should be appreciated that players of this caliber were already proficient to an incredible degree in orthodox play before they aspired to more sensational methods. The prime function of every pass is that it should arrive at the appointed place at the opportune moment and it follows that the good player will possess all-round passing ability.

In passing, accuracy is far more important than speed and the beginner should aim to pass the ball to the receiver so that he can receive it at approximately chest height; from this position the receiver can immediately pass, start a dribble or make a shot at the basket with the minimum waste of time. Later, as play develops, there will be exceptions to this principle. For example, on occasions it may be advisable to pass the ball so that it is taken above head height, enabling the receiver to execute immediately a two-handed overhead shot; in this instance a pass at chest height would cause unnecessary waste of time and effort.

No team or player can have too much passing practice and in the learning stages straightforward passing and catching drills in which two or more players pass the ball to each other by the prescribed method will enable the coach to teach the essen-tials. As skill and experience improve the drills can be made more and more related to the game situations.

Contrary to popular belief, far more fumbles and failures in ball handling are due to faulty passing than to poor catching, though there is a tendency for complete novices to <u>fight</u> the ball when it comes to them. If the coach insists on accuracy in the passing practices good catching will soon become second nature to the players as long as they are taught to take the ball in the finger tips (*not* with the palms), letting the fingers, wrists and arms <u>give</u> as contact is made. They should also move in to receive the pass.

At no time in basketball can a blind pass be condoned but this does not mean that the receiver must always be directly in front of the passer. By using peripheral vision, which allows a person to see beyond his direct line of focus, it is possible to pass the ball with accuracy over a wide angle of view without turning the head. Once the fundamental techniques of passing have been learned, players should try to make full use of their peripheral vision so that they avoid <u>telegraphing</u> to the opponents the direction of the intended pass. Faking and feinting must also be integral parts of passing technique but these aids will be discussed later.

As a final generalization on passing it is often said that two hands are better than one, but there are occasions when a one-handed pass is to be preferred, as will be seen later. When the player comes to equip himself with these one-handed passes he should aim at being equally adept with either hand; therefore as soon as the particular pass has been learned with the natural hand, practice must be devoted to gaining proficiency with the other hand. Incidentally, in the interests of simplicity, all descriptions for one-handed passes refer to the use of the right hand; those for the left hand can be readily deduced.

Two-Handed Chest Pass

(Diagram 3)

This is undoubtedly the basic pass of basketball and one that should be the beginner's main method of moving the ball about the court. Even with the most experienced players it is used more than any other single type of pass.

The ball is held in front of the body at chest height with the arms partially bent and the elbows fairly low. The hands are placed on the sides of the ball, slightly to the rear, and it is controlled by the fingers and thumbs which are well spread to cover as much of the surface as possible. The pass is made by extending the arms and snapping the wrists to push the ball towards the target. The snap of the wrists is the secret of a good chest pass and it helps if beginners concentrate on turning the palms outwards (so that the thumbs are pointing downwards) as the ball is released.

DIAGRAM 3

The chest pass is the safest and simplest way of passing the ball over short distances whenever a direct pass is possible.

Two-Handed Bounce Pass

(Diagram 4)

This is another useful pass that can be readily learned by the beginner and one which will prove a valuable asset throughout his playing career. It is a complement to the chest pass and is used to prevent possible interception that might occur if a direct pass were used. The bounce pass is particularly useful in helping to penetrate a zone defense, to feed a pivot player or to beat a tall player who dominates the higher passing levels.

The technique of the bounce pass is similar to that of the chest pass except that the ball is released from hip level with a more pronounced arm action and pushed into the floor so that it rebounds into the receiver's hands. This stronger arm action

is necessary because the ball quickly loses its momentum after striking the floor. Care must be taken to direct the ball at a point on the floor nearer to the receiver than to the passer, otherwise it may never reach him.

Two-Handed Overhead Pass

This is a high-level pass that is particularly useful for tall players but can be used effectively by anyone who receives the ball above head height and wants to make a quick pass to a teammate. The ball should be held above the head with the arms slightly bent and the fingers and thumbs spread along the sides and rear of the ball. The ball is propelled by a sharp extension of the arms and a snap of the wrists and fingers as before but with very little follow-through of the arms. When correctly executed it is a very fast pass and difficult to intercept.

Baseball Pass

(Diagram 5)

Also known as the Javelin Pass, it is the ideal method of combining distance and speed and is invaluable for initiating fast breaks. It is not one that should be introduced too early to beginners as they tend to be rather wild and erratic when using one hand.

The ball should be taken quickly with both hands to a position by the side of the head over the right shoulder and at the same time the left leg is moved forward in the general

DIAGRAM 5

direction of the intended pass. The left hand is removed and the ball taken still further back behind the shoulder, with the thumb and fingers well spread, and then whipped through with an elbow and wrist action. The body, arm and fingers should all follow through in the direction of the pass. Lack of control is usually caused by a failure to keep both hands on the ball in the initial phase or is due to the thrower taking the ball too wide of the head as the pass is made.

One-Handed Cross-Over Bounce Pass

(Diagram 6)

Here is a pass that is similar in function to the two-handed bounce pass but which can be used to get the ball past an intervening opponent to a colleague who would otherwise be blocked out. It can prove most effective in passing to a pivot player who is well placed for taking a shot.

If the pass is to be made to the right of the intervening guard, the thrower makes a long cross-over step with the left

DIAGRAM 6

leg and takes the ball well out to the right side with both hands. From this position, which gives the ball maximum protection, the left hand is removed and the ball thrown into the floor beyond the guard so that it rebounds into the receiver's hands. An almost straight arm action is used with the fingers well spread behind the ball to give additional push. There should be a good follow through.

Hook Pass
(Diagram 7)

This is another one-handed pass that can be used to propel the ball past an intervening guard and is best used when the player is facing forwards and wishes to throw the ball sideways to a teammate. When used by tall players it is virtually unstoppable, and is no less effective with most players if combined with a jump, because of the high trajectory of the ball. The technique should be learned first of all without incorporating a jump.

When making the pass the thrower turns his body so that the left shoulder is directed towards the receiver and sweeps the ball out to the right side with both hands. Then, continuing the sweep of the ball, the left hand is removed and the ball brought with a straight arm action vertically above the head from where it is released with a wrist and finger action so that it is directed at the receiver. There is little or no follow-through.

Common errors when learning the hook pass are a failure to turn the head towards the receiver before releasing the ball and a tendency to use a bent arm action. Both of these faults lead to inaccuracy and should be checked from the outset.

DIAGRAM 7

Although there are innumerable other ways of passing the ball these six methods constitute the fundamental passes of the game and are the ones that should be mastered by every player so that he has sufficient all-round passing ability to meet most situations that may arise. Whatever passes may be developed at a later date, most of them will be merely variations and adaptations of the techniques involved in these six methods. In this respect mention should also be made of the Scoop and Give type of passes that feature prominently in the play of the experts. As the names imply, the ball is almost handed to the receiver rather than passed to him and little actual technique is involved; they are more a matter of quick reaction allied to game experience.

PASSING DRILLS

Having learned the correct technique of the various passes by straightforward passing and catching of the ball, the coach should devise drills to increase the scope of the practice so that the players can perfect the techniques they have learned. The following examples are typical drills that can be used for this purpose. As they do not involve shooting or dribbling the coach can concentrate all his attention on developing good passing and catching technique. Later, as the players become more proficient, the passing drills can combine the various handling techniques.

1. Pass and Follow

One ball between 6 to 8 players who form up in a fairly large circle (somewhere in the region of 20 feet in diameter). The player with the ball passes it to another member of the circle, but not to an immediate neighbor, and then follows up the pass to take the place of the receiver who will himself have passed the ball and followed on. This is a most useful drill for beginners as they must keep the ball moving and must break as soon as the pass has been made. The two-handed chest, bounce and overhead passes can all be used in this drill.

2. Two Ball Passing

Two players, each with a ball, stand facing a third player some 15 to 20 feet away. Using different types of passes the two players feed their colleague as rapidly as possible but ensuring he never receives the second ball until he has returned the other one to the passer. This drill demands speed and accuracy in passing and, by moving the two feeders wider apart, encourages the third player to use his peripheral vision.

3. Post Passing

(Diagram 8)

Four players take up the corner positions of a square and a fifth player stands in the center. The ball is passed from player to player always following the same path as

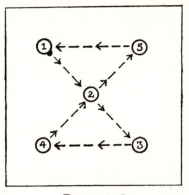

DIAGRAM 8

shown in the diagram. All methods of passing can be used and if the ball is kept moving it is an excellent type of passing drill for the center player in particular. Players should take turns at being the center man.

As skill improves a second ball can be introduced into the drill, thus making it more difficult; the second ball follows precisely the same path but is one pass behind.

4. File Passing

(Diagram 9)

Two files of three or four players line up as shown in the

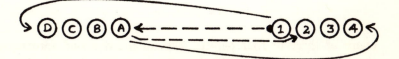

DIAGRAM 9

diagram. Player 1 passes to A, follows up the ball and cuts through to join the end of the opposite file. In the meantime A has passed to player 2 and followed through and the drill continues in this way. This drill is particularly useful for developing speed and accuracy in the basic two-handed chest pass and cultivating the habit of moving in to receive the ball.

5. Give and Go

(Diagram 10)

A rather tricky drill at first but one which adds variety and enjoyment and gives practice to a wide range of skills. Four

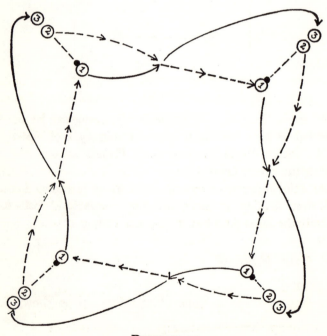

DIAGRAM 10

teams of three or four players take up the diamond formation shown in the diagram. Number 1 in each team has a ball and faces the other men. On a starting signal from the coach each number 1 passes the ball to his number 2 and then runs towards the next corner (clockwise or counterclockwise as prescribed by the coach). He receives a return pass from his own number 2 and immediately passes it to the number 2 of the next corner, who has moved forward to the original position of number 1, and joins the end of that file. The drill continues as before, number 2 passing to number 3 and then running towards the next corner. All methods of passing can be used in this drill and the coach should indicate the three passes he wants. These can be varied at the coach's discretion. Among other factors, passing the ball to a moving player and receiving the ball on the run are emphasized in this drill.

DRIBBLING

The focal point of basketball is at all times the ball and there is a danger of inexperienced players dribbling the ball unnecessarily in order to associate themselves with the game. Prolonged contact with the ball may give immense pleasure to the individual but to be functional in the team play dribbling must always have a purpose.

It would be unwise to state categorically when dribbling should or should not be used as so much depends upon the particular situation at the time. Some coaches advocate that the ball should never be dribbled if a pass is possible but this policy seems rather unimaginative. There are many occasions when a dribble can be used to advantage and many situations when it is to be preferred to a pass, and each one must be judged on its merits. The following headings give some guidance as to when dribbling may be the correct tactics to employ but it is far from comprehensive and certainly not compulsory.

1. To get clear of a pressing opponent.
2. To draw the opposing defense away from a particular area.
3. To get the ball away from a congested area.

4. To move to a better position for setting up an attacking play.

5. To set up a screen for a teammate.

6. To prevent contact or travelling violations when taking the ball on the move.

7. To drive into the basket for a shot when a screen has been set up.

8. To drive past a close guarding opponent after he has been successfully faked.

9. To advance the ball up the court, especially on a fast breaking attack.

10. To slow down the tempo of play as part of a team strategy.

When used intelligently under these, and other, circumstances the dribble can play a vital part in basketball but it can be a menace when used merely as a habit. Players must avoid dribbling the ball automatically each time they receive it (a fault common with beginners); otherwise they will hold up play more times than they contribute to it. Another habit to be avoided is the one bounce dribble where the player bounces the ball once and immediately recatches it without moving from his position on the floor. This action achieves nothing for it does not even move the ball from one position on the court to another and often means that the player misses an opportunity of making a quick pass or shot at the basket. Furthermore, having made the one bounce dribble the player has deprived himself of the right to move to another position on the floor with the ball, thus restricting his attacking potential and making his opponent's task much easier.

Because dribbling has a definite function in the game, players must be as proficient in this skill as in the other handling fundamentals of passing and shooting, even though dribbling is never used to the same extent. Diligent practice is the only way to master this rather spectacular skill and though the amount of time devoted to practice may seem out of proportion to its value in the game, dribbling is an excellent means of promoting general handling ability and familiarity with the ball. The various drills and exercises used to perfect dribbling technique will do much to improve the beginner's confidence and help him to become a more competent player.

Needless to say, a good dribbler is equally adept with either hand so that he can move in any direction and not expose the ball to danger. The good dribbler always uses the hand furthest away from possible interception so that maximum protection is given to the ball. By giving equal emphasis to the use of either hand in the practices the coach will make sure his players do not become one-hand dribblers.

Technique of Dribbling

The ball is not hit or slapped by the palm of the hand but is pushed into the floor by the finger tips with a caressing action of the wrist and fingers. Control is assisted by a cushioning action of the whole arm so that the fingers ride with the ball. When maximum protection is essential (to draw the opposing defense away from the area) the ball is bounced at approximately knee height usually to the side, with the body well over the ball so that it is shielded from any guarding opponent. If there is no danger of interception and speed is required (to move the ball up the court in a fast attack) the ball is pushed into the floor ahead of the dribbler so that it bounces between waist and shoulder height, enabling him to advance with an almost normal running action. There is no restriction on the number of paces that can be taken to each bounce of the ball and when dribbling at speed it is possible to cover a considerable distance with very few bounces. Even a small player can get right up to the basket from well outside the free throw lane with but a couple of bounces, a scoring potential that is often ignored.

Having learned the essentials of dribbling technique, players must combine them with the different aspects of footwork so that legal stopping with the ball, change of pace and direction and ability to pass or shoot the ball on the move without violating the travelling laws all become second nature to them. They must also be able to dribble the ball with complete control without actually looking at it so that they are fully aware of the situations around them.

DRIBBLING DRILLS

Dribbling, like shooting, is a fundamental that the player can practice entirely on his own and good players spend a great deal of time improving their ability in this quarter by making the most of every available spare moment. No amount of solo practice will accustom the player to using this skill under game conditions so suitable drills must be employed. These five examples give practice to dribbling, without involving shooting, under varying conditions. Where necessary, drills can be conducted at walking pace to begin with and then speeded up.

1. Three Man Dribble

Two players stand one behind the other at one end of the court, the front person holding the ball, and their colleague stands at the other end of the court. Player number 1 dribbles down the court, gives the ball to number 2 and takes his place. Number 2 dribbles the ball back down the court, gives it to the third player and the drill continues in this way. This is a simple drill but is one that is very useful in the initial stages for allowing the coach to check basic technique. While the drill is in progress he can shout instructions to the dribbler to change hands, dribble at speed, dribble defensively, and so on.

2. Obstacle Dribbling

In a variation of the above drill, players dribble the ball up and down the court as before but weaving in and out of obstacles (boxes, chairs, etc.) that have been placed at intervals. The obstacles must be visualized as opponents and the appropriate defensive action taken.

3. Truck and Trailer

One of the fundamental drills of basketball. One player dribbles the ball a distance up the court, executes a legal stop, pivots and then passes the ball to his partner who has been following up a short distance behind. The new handler now dribbles the ball, his partner becomes trailer and the drill continues. This simple drill is excellent practice for combining dribbling, footwork and passing.

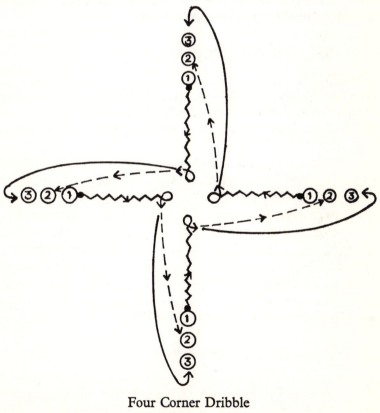

Four Corner Dribble

DIAGRAM 11

4. *Four Corner Dribble*

(Diagram 11)

Teams of three or four players, the front one holding a ball, line up in diamond formation (as shown in the diagram). On a signal from the coach each number 1 dribbles towards the center, executes a legal stop, pivots in the direction that has already been indicated by the coach and then passes the ball to number 2 of the next corner. Number 1 follows his pass to join the end of that file, number 2 dribbles towards the center and the drill continues. This is another useful drill that combines dribbling, passing and footwork.

5. *Pick Up and Dribble*

(Diagram 12)

Four or five players form an arc (see Diagram 12), standing approximately two yards apart, with player A holding the ball. Player A rolls the ball on the floor along an imaginary radius

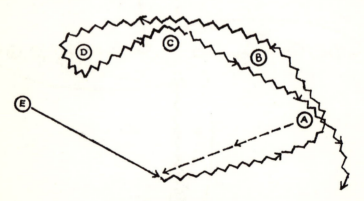

DIAGRAM 12

of the arc and player E runs forward, scoops up the ball and immediately begins to dribble it. He dribbles round the back of the arc and then weaves in and out of the players until he is in a position beyond A. Player E then rolls the ball along

40

the floor, D runs out to collect it and the drill continues. Once again the correct hand must be used at all times.

The drill can be made more objective if the players in the arc try to <u>steal</u> the ball as the dribbler weaves in and out but they must not move their feet in doing so, otherwise the drill will break down.

3 *Individual Skills (2)*
Shooting

AS THE ultimate object of basketball is to get the ball into the basket, there is hardly any necessity to impress upon players the importance of shooting. Most of them realize it is the team which scores the most baskets that wins the game! Consequently there is usually a greater readiness to devote time to practicing this fundamental than to any other phase of basketball skill. In any case, whether in practice or match play, shooting is enjoyable and satisfying because there is always tangible evidence on which to judge the success or otherwise of the efforts made.

Many players have what is commonly called a <u>good eye</u> for shooting and seem to take naturally to the various shooting techniques once they have acquired a degree of general ball-handling ability. With correct teaching and sufficient practice most players can become competent at shooting and it is imperative that every individual player do his utmost to reach this standard. Every player must consider himself as a potential shooter whenever his team is in possession of the ball. Admittedly, it is usual for a team to have one or two specialists who score the majority of the baskets and the pattern of team attack will tend to bring these players into scoring opportunities more often than the other men. However, many certain scoring opportunities will be lost if a team does not have all-round shooting prowess but has to rely on getting the ball to the specialists. Moreover, if any player is not a potential scoring threat his opponents need not guard him closely and this may well allow them to concentrate their defense upon the known danger men and so play them out of the game by <u>double teaming</u> tactics. Other things being equal, the nearer to the basket that the shot is made the greater is its chance of success and the good team will always work the ball into the best scoring position and not necessarily to a particular player.

As with dribbling, shooting is enjoyable and to a certain extent spectacular; therefore it can easily be misused by inexperienced players in their eagerness to participate in the play. In actual fact, very few players accurately evaluate their own shooting efficiency. In principle, a shot should never be attempted unless it has at least a 50-50 chance of success, yet how often one sees even experienced players attempting a shot that they would seldom <u>sink</u> even in practice when there is no pressure upon them. Any player who congratulates himself at the end of a game simply because he has scored more baskets than any of his colleagues is misguided to say the least. The points on the scoresheet only tell part of the story for they do not indicate the number of baskets that have been missed! Only by calculating the percentage of successful shots in relation to the number of attempts made can a true picture of shooting ability be derived. Many efficient coaches keep individual Shooting Charts on all their players so that after each game there is a detailed record of every shot attempted, whether made or missed. These charts are often highly elaborate, showing not only a numerical tally of all shots attempted but also recording such information as the type of shot, the precise position on the floor from where it was taken, which hand if it was one-handed, what action preceded the shot and so on. From all this evidence the coach can determine the player's percentage for each specific phase and can regulate his practice accordingly in order to improve those aspects that do not come up to the required standard. Quite obviously this is a very complicated system and requires a team of recorders to tabulate all the information.

Name of Player	JOHN SMITH											Season			
	SHORT SHOTS			MEDIUM SHOTS			LONG SHOTS			MATCH TOTALS					
OPPONENTS	ATTEMPTS	TOTAL	MADE	%	ATTEMPTS	TOTAL	MADE	%	ATTEMPTS	TOTAL	MADE	%	TOTAL ATPS.	TOTAL MADE	FINAL %
TIGERS	✓✓x ✓✓x✓ x✓x	10	6	60	xx✓x ✓✓x ✓	8	4	50	x✓xx✓x	6	2	$33\frac{1}{3}$	24	12	50
SEASON TOTALS															

AN INDIVIDUAL SHOOTING CHART

DIAGRAM 13

In the interests of improving shooting ability any type of Shooting Chart, no matter how simple, is of value if only to prove to the player that his percentage is not as high as it should be, thus encouraging him to practice harder. The one shown in Diagram 13 is an example of a simplified Shooting Chart which could well be used by most clubs to record a player's percentages. Here the shots are classified as short, medium and long (see Diagram 14) which is sufficient to give the players an accurate guide to their shooting proficiency.

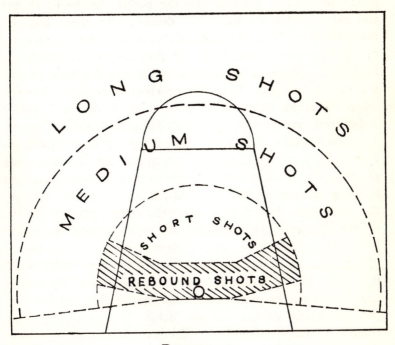

DIAGRAM 14

TECHNIQUE OF SHOOTING

There is an imposing array of different methods of shooting used in basketball by the expert player and, as with passing, many are designed for use in specific situations. Such factors as position on the court, distance from the basket, proximity of opponents, the play preceding the shot and many other considerations can all influence the type of shot to be used. As previously indicated, the beginner should concentrate on the two basic shots of the game rather than try to master too many too soon, but once these have been accomplished and the general principles of shooting grasped, the aim of every player should be to develop all-round shooting ability.

The first question with regard to technique is in relation to the use of the backboard. It is quite permissible for the player to rebound the ball into the basket via the backboard and many people are under the delusion that most shots are made this way. In good basketball this is not so for the majority of shots are made directly at the ring and do not touch the backboard. It would be unwise to be too dogmatic in this matter but, as a general rule, the backboard should only be used when the player drives in to make a lay-up shot or is taking a shot from anywhere within the shaded area shown in Diagram 14. When making this type of shot the player should focus his eyes on the point of rebound and not on the ring. From all other points on the court a direct shot is to be preferred, the player focusing his eyes on the ring and aiming to get the ball over the front edge. It is easy to select the correct point of contact on the backboard for a rebound shot when close to the basket but it becomes far more difficult from further out because the player must adjust his shot according to the angle from which it is taken as well as his distance from the basket. By making the shot direct the player eliminates one variable and can concentrate purely on the distance factor. If anything, a player should overshoot rather than undershoot when making a direct shot, for invariably undershooting results in the ball falling tamely out of court or into the opponents' hands. Ideally, of course, the player should hit the happy medium so that the ball drops straight into the basket!

The flight of the ball is another important consideration in the technique of shooting. Theoretically, the more vertical the descent of the ball the greater is its chance of entering the ring because a larger target is presented (see Diagram 15), and it would seem that this is an argument in favor of giving a very high trajectory to the ball. However, this must be related

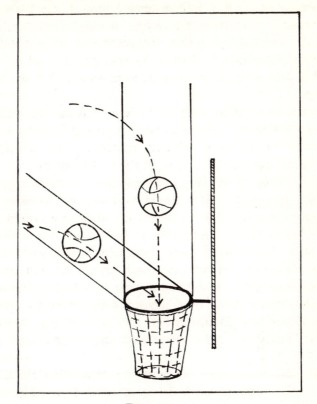

DIAGRAM 15

to the fact that the greater the distance travelled by the ball the more is the chance of error; therefore the best flight is a compromise of these two elements. In time, every player will discover his own individual compromise through experimentation but when learning the different shots plenty of flight should be given to the ball rather than a flat trajectory.

As with all the other handling skills, the wrists and fingers play a prominent part in the technique of shooting. No matter what type of shot is being used the ball is released from the fingertips with a strong wrist and finger action and in most instances there is a good follow-through on release of the ball, the arm or arms being fully extended towards the basket and the eyes still focused on the target. A blind shot must never be made. Even though a shot may commence while the player has his back towards the basket, he must get his head and eyes round to look at the target as soon as possible before the ball is released.

So far, no mention has been made of spin and this omission has been deliberate. The beginner has enough to cope with in the matter of technique without introducing the question of spin, which is of doubtful value at the best of times.

In all phases of shooting technique the acid test must surely be Is it successful? If a player is hitting the necessary percentage using rebound shots when, according to accepted principles, he should be using direct shots, then his method is vindicated. Similarly, if other unorthodox techniques are producing the desired results the coach should let him develop his individual style. Good form alone is not the criterion of good shooting; it must be combined with percentage success. Before individual interpretations are encouraged, however, players should learn and practice according to the correct techniques.

The following types of shots are those that should be mastered by every player if he is to have all-round shooting ability. Repeated practice at these various techniques will enable him to become a competent shooter but this does not necessarily mean that he will be a good scorer in competitive match play. So much can depend upon a player's temperament; determination and confidence can play as great a part as actual shooting ability. A consistent player of moderate ability with the will to win may prove a far better scoring proposition than a technically superior colleague who lacks fighting spirit or is easily upset.

It is neither reasonable nor desirable to try to list all the different shots used in the game. Those included below represent the main scoring weapons and the majority of those omitted are merely variations or modifications of these and will ultimately be developed quite naturally by players once they are proficient in the fundamental shots. Once again, descriptions of one-handed techniques refer to the use of the right hand.

Lay-Up Shot

(Diagram 16)

The lay-up shot is a short distance rebound shot usually made on the move following a dribble or a running catch. The pronounced improvement in medium and long distance techniques has somewhat reduced the prominence of the lay-up shot in present day basketball, but it should still be regarded as the most important action shot in the game. After all, in every attacking move there should be the underlying objective of getting the ball as near to the basket as possible before making the shot, and the ultimate of this is achieved in the lay-up shot. It is a difficult shot for the beginner to master as it requires good co-ordination, timing and judgment; but once learned, it is the easiest to perform well.

DIAGRAM 16

When approaching the basket from the right-hand side the player makes an upward jump from the left foot and at the same time carries the ball up in front of the body with both hands until it is above the head. Just before the peak of the jump the left hand is removed and the right arm extended to place the ball against the backboard, some 6-10 inches above the ring, and slightly to the side, so that it rebounds into the basket. The essence of a good lay-up shot is for the player to gain maximum height after taking off at the correct distance from the basket, and to release the ball from a fully extended position of the body and arm at the peak of the jump so that it travels the minimum distance possible. The ball brushes against the backboard rather than striking it. If the approach is made from the left side of the basket, the shot is made with the left hand from a right-footed take-off.

Understandably beginners do not find the execution of a good lay-up shot easy because they have insufficient skill to co-ordinate the handling of the ball with correct judgment of take-off point and selection of the rebound spot. The result is they invariably find themselves either taking off from too far out and having to throw the ball at the backboard, or they leave it too late and find themselves beneath the basket and unable to make a shot at all. When first learning the lay-up shot the beginner should stand some five or six feet away from the basket, at an angle of approximately 45 degrees, holding the ball in front of the chest with both hands and with the eyes focused on the rebound spot. He then takes one pace with the left leg, at the same time carrying the ball up in front of the face, and as the foot strikes the floor he makes an upward jump to release the ball against the rebound spot from the extended position previously described. The eyes are focused on the backboard throughout the movement. From this simple beginning the player can gradually build up the rhythm of the action by dribbling slowly towards the basket, collecting the ball so that the left foot hits the take-off point on the second count of the permitted two beats and then executing the shot as before. As co-ordination and confidence increase the speed of approach can be stepped up until eventually the lay-up shot is being performed at full speed. The faster the approach the further out will be the ideal point of take-off but players will, with experience, adjust this to suit themselves.

Two-Handed Set Shot

(Diagram 17)
This is probably the most natural and readily mastered shot for beginners, particularly if they have had ample passing practice before being introduced to shooting techniques, because it is a logical development of the two-handed chest pass. It is a general utility shot that is made from a standing position when the player is not closely guarded or has faked his guard off balance. It is best used at a distance of 10-20 feet.

DIAGRAM 17

The ball is held in front of the body with both hands more or less as for the start of the chest pass; the feet can be side by side or one in front of the other, whichever stance feels more comfortable, and there is a slight forward lean. The eyes are focused on the target. At the commencement of the shot, the ball is dropped slightly and the knees are partially bent. The shot is continued by bringing the ball up in front of the face as the legs are straightened; the arms are extended above the head to release the ball with a snap of the wrists. The eyes do not follow the flight of the ball but remain fixed on the target. A common error with beginners is to shoot the ball forward at the target instead of bringing the ball up close to the face.

One-Handed Set Shot

(Diagram 18)

Once the technique of the two-handed set shot has been mastered, players will find little difficulty in adding the one-handed version to their repertoire. It can be used in precisely

DIAGRAM 18

the same way as the two-handed shot and players may find that they prefer to use this method; it is a matter of individual choice. If the set shot must be taken quickly, the one-handed method is undoubtedly the better technique and for this reason it is an excellent scoring weapon when a player has dribbled towards the basket, come to a rapid stop and wishes to take a shot without delay.

The ball is held at shoulder height in front of the body in both hands but with the right hand to the rear of the ball. The position of the feet is optional but most players prefer to have one foot in front of the other (usually the right) as it seems to assist balance. Keeping the weight forward, the ball is brought up to head height with the shooting hand dropped back and the knees are partially bent. The left hand is removed and the ball is pushed upwards towards the basket by straightening the legs and extending the arm; the wrist gives a final flick to the ball as it leaves the fingertips.

Two-Handed Overhead Shot

This is a shot generally preferred by tall players but is one that can be usefully employed by everyone when fairly close to the basket. Quite often a player will receive a pass, take a rebound from the backboard, or make an interception at or above head height when in a favorable shooting position. In these circumstances an immediate shot from above the head can result in a basket whereas the delay incurred by adjusting for a normal set shot may well enable an opponent to block it.

The shot commences with the ball held above the head with the arms partially bent; the hands are underneath the ball with the fingers spread. The ball is pushed upwards towards the basket by extending the arms and snapping the wrists strongly. There is a good follow-through of the fingers on completion of the shot which should finish with the backs of the hands close together and the thumbs pointing downwards to the floor. Additional distance can be obtained by using a bending and straightening action of the legs as in the set shots, but as this is essentially a short range shot such measures are seldom needed.

One-Handed Overhead Shot

From the previous action it is a simple matter to develop the one-handed method. Normally players tend to use either one or the other method as there is little advantage to be gained from perfecting two shots of identical purpose. Nevertheless beginners should learn and practice both methods so that they can discover which one is best suited to them and then cultivate it.

The ball is held above the head in both hands with the right hand underneath it and the left hand supporting it at the front. The arms are partially bent. The left hand is removed and the ball is pushed upwards towards the basket as before by extending the arm and snapping the wrist strongly.

The Hook Shot

(Diagram 19)

This is a most spectacular looking shot and in the hands of an expert pivot player can be one of the most devastating of scoring

DIAGRAM 19

weapons. Like its counterpart, the hook pass, it is virtually unstoppable. It should really be regarded as a short range shot though many players who specialize in this method of shooting can obtain remarkable accuracy from further out. In spite of its spectacular appearance it is considered technically easier than some of the others already discussed and every player should regard it as a fundamental method of shooting. The tall player should place it high on his priority list.

The shot commences with the back towards the basket and the ball is held in front of the player so that the body is shielding it from any guarding opponent. It can be taken from a standing position or, as is more usual, following a step away from the guard to give more latitude. The step is made with the left foot and the ball is swept up in front of the body as in the hook pass. As the ball is swept up the left shoulder is directed at the basket and the head is turned to look at the target with the body leaning slightly towards it. The ball continues its arc, the left hand is removed and the ball released from vertically over the head. The right leg is allowed to swing through and the shot is made from the left foot. Some players leap from the floor as the shot is made in order to gain additional height but if the correct timing and action are used this is hardly necessary. Experienced players can execute a hook shot on the move while cutting across the court. This is an advanced technique and one that should not be introduced to beginners.

Turn-Around Shot

Strictly speaking this is not a different shot; it is merely a particular application of the one- or two-handed overhead shots. Like the hook shot it starts with the back towards the basket and is a vital technique for the pivot player. It is used most frequently from a position just outside the free throw lane on either side of the basket.

Holding the ball in front of him at chest height, the player suddenly turns to face the basket by pivoting on one foot, simultaneously bringing the ball up above the head with both hands. From here a normal one- or two-handed overhead shot can be made at the basket. The turn-around is often preceded by a fake in the opposite direction to the actual turn to put the opposing guard off balance. Many experienced players prefer to use the one-handed method on turn-around shots as they feel they can get greater accuracy and at the same time afford more protection to the ball. This is very much a matter for the individual to decide but when learning the technique it is best for the beginner to use the two-handed method because this is easier to control. It is also essential that players should be able to make the turn-around in either direction so that the shot cannot be anticipated by the guard.

Jump Shot

(Diagram 20)

No other single skill has had as great effect upon the balance of defensive and attacking play as the development of the jump shot. The high scoring rates in first-class basketball today can nearly always be attributed to proficiency of players in this department. It is a formidable shot that can be made from any-

DIAGRAM 20

where on the court within scoring range and against which there is no defense. It can be made from a standing position, or, as is more effective, at the end of a dribble.

When following a dribble, the player comes to a sudden stop at the required place with the feet close together and the ball held in front of the body with both hands. The knees are bent slightly in preparation for the jump. This same starting position is used if the shot is made from standing. A high upward jump is made from both feet and the ball is carried above the head with the right hand folded back underneath the ball and the left hand supporting it at the front. The shooting arm is crooked at approximately a right angle. The left hand is removed and the ball is released with a sharp extension of the arm and snap of the wrist. It is a vital part of the jump shot technique that the release should not be made while the body is still rising but should occur at the peak of the jump or even a little afterwards. This correct timing is the secret of a good jump shot and gives the illusion that the player hangs momentarily in the air as the shot is executed.

In addition to faulty timing of the actual release, a common error with beginners is to make the jump forwards instead of vertically upwards. In actual fact many expert players develop a fall-away technique in their jump shooting so that they jump slightly backwards to get clear of a close guarding opponent. The jump shot is a fairly advanced shooting technique and should only be learned after the player has mastered the other fundamental shots. Plenty of practice and coaching will be required before he becomes a consistent jump shooter.

Free–Throw Shot

(Diagram 21)

That games are frequently won or lost on free throws should be continually impressed upon players. In any match that is decided by but a few points the winning team may well have gained its victory due to its ability to make good any free throws awarded. Equally, a team that fails to register any points with its free throws is jeopardizing its chance of winning. A free throw at the basket eliminates all the variables that normally apply in shooting because the distance is constant, the player can select

DIAGRAM 21

his precise position and his method of shooting, and there is no interference from the opponents. In professional basketball a free throw is invariably a gift of one point; with practice there is no reason why it should not be the same for all teams.

Opinions vary as to the type of shot to be used for a free throw. Some coaches argue that players should use their regular set shot method rather than employ a specific free throw technique. To support this viewpoint it is claimed that an additional method increases the number of skills to be practiced. By using the one type of shot for both purposes the player can devote the same amount of practice time to perfecting just one technique. On the other hand some coaches advocate the use of the two-handed underhand shot for free throws as they feel players can achieve greater accuracy by this method. This shot has no place in normal floor play but if it brings a high percentage of success at free throws, practice at it has been justified.

In the two-handed underhand shot the player stands with the feet astride, immediately behind the free throw line, and the ball is held in front of the body with the arms almost straight. The fingers are spread along the sides of the ball and slightly underneath it. Keeping the back straight and the eyes focused on the ring, the knees are bent and the arms lowered to bring the ball between the knees. From here the arms are brought up and forwards as the knees are straightened and the ball is released at approximately shoulder level so that it is lobbed over the front edge of the ring. There should be a good follow-through with the arms, and the body rises up on the toes.

Only time will show a player which is his most successful method for taking a free throw but he should learn and practice this method before making the decision. Practicing free throw shooting is not as exciting as the other phases of shooting skill but the coach should allocate part of every training session to this fundamental of the game. It is always infuriating to have to admit that a game was lost because of missed free throws.

SHOOTING DRILLS

Once the essentials of the different shooting techniques have been learned through individual practice and coaching, the use of drills will accustom the players to applying their shooting ability under game conditions. The following examples of shooting drills combine the various handling skills but do not involve complicated tactics. Many others can be devised.

1. Two–Shot Drill

Players pair off, each one with a ball. Player 1 stands facing the basket in a shooting position some 10 to 15 feet away while his partner takes up a position close to the basket. Number 1 attempts a straightforward set shot (one or two-handed as preferred) and immediately receives a pass from number 2. He must then make a quick shot with the second ball before number 2, who has followed up his pass, can block him out. The two players change roles frequently. This is an excellent drill for practicing normal set shooting and set shooting under pressure. It can also be used for practice of the overhead shot if the second ball is received at the appropriate height.

2. Lay-Up Drill

(Diagram 22)

This is probably the best-known and most often used of all basketball drills, and is of immense value. It enables a lot of players to get plenty of activity in a short time and as such is an excellent warming-up drill. In addition, it is an ideal way of practicing the lay-up shot with a large group of players when only one ball is available.

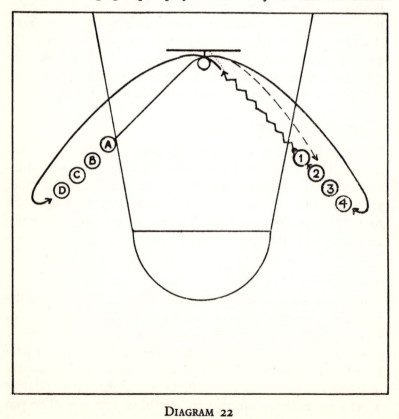

DIAGRAM 22

The players form up in two files as shown in Diagram 22. Player 1 dribbles the ball towards the basket, makes a lay-up shot and continues running to join the end of the opposite file. As soon as number 1 has made his shot, player A runs in to retrieve the ball, passes it out to number 2 who immediately dribbles in for a lay-up shot. Player A then joins the end of the other file. The drill continues in this way, the right-hand file always making the shot while the left hand file acts as retrievers. The sequence can be reversed so that the players practice driving in from the left side and making the lay-up with the left hand.

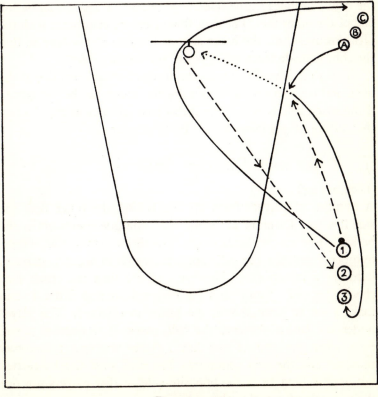

DIAGRAM 23

Passing, shooting, dribbling and general handling ability are all put to the test in this drill and experienced players can work up a tremendous tempo so that it is a most impressive drill to watch.

3. *Cut and Shooting Drill*

(Diagram 23)

Players form up in two files as shown in Diagram 23, with number 1 holding the ball. Player A cuts to a pivot position just outside the free throw lane, receives a pass from number 1 and immediately executes a hook or turn-around shot. Player 1 runs through to retrieve the ball, passes it out to number 2 and the drill continues in the same way. Players 1 and A join on the end of the other file. The drill should also be conducted with the files positioned on the other side of the free throw lane so that the shot is made from the opposite side of the court.

This drill is well suited to the straightforward practice of the hook and turn-around shots but greater reality can be brought in if the coach stands in the free throw lane and acts as guard when the cutting player takes up the pivot position.

4. *Drive and Shooting Drill*

(Diagram 24)

A number of players form up one behind the other near the side line (see Diagram 24) while one colleague stands under the basket. The coach stands in the free throw semi-circle. Player number 1 dribbles the ball round the coach in order to drive in hard for a lay-up shot. However, at any time the coach may shout Set or Jump and the player must stop instantly and make a set or jump shot at the basket as directed. The player under the basket retrieves the ball, passes it to number 2 and then joins the end of the line. Player number 1 becomes retriever and the drill continues. The drill must also be carried out approaching from the opposite side so that players practice their shooting from all angles.

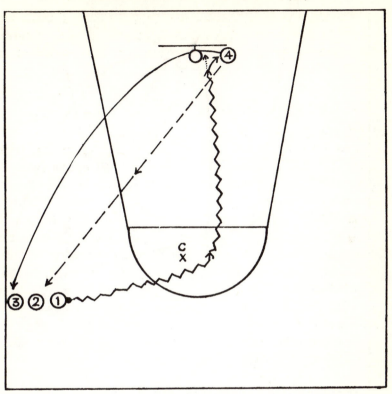

DIAGRAM 24

5. *Three–Man Shooting Drill*

(Diagram 25)

Players line up in three files as shown in Diagram 25, with number 1 holding the ball. Player 1 passes to player A, who has broken to a pivot position by the free throw lane, and then runs through to a post position in the semi-circle. At the same time player X cuts round him and receives a pass from A. Having received the ball he can stop and make a jump or set shot, drive through for a lay-up, or pass to number 1 for him to make the shot. Player A retrieves the ball and passes it to number 2 so that the next threesome can continue the drill. The three who have

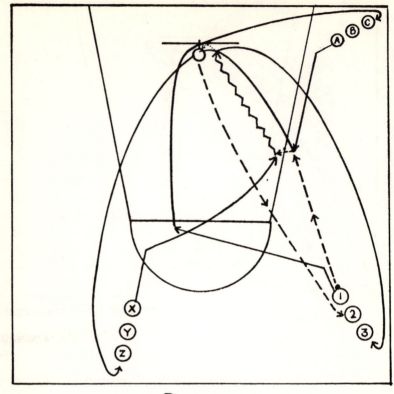

DIAGRAM 25

just completed the sequence join the end of the next file moving along in a counterclockwise direction.

This drill gives the players more scope in deciding the shot to be used and is an excellent combination practice of passing and shooting. The drill must also be conducted with the pivot line on the opposite side of the basket so that the shooting techniques are practiced from the other side of the court.

4 *Principles of Defense*

IN RECENT years attacking play has far outstripped defensive methods, due principally to vastly improved shooting techniques. The accuracy of some of the players in first-class basketball today is nothing short of miraculous; they can hit percentages of 75 and over without extending themselves. In particular, the development of the jump shot has, to a certain extent, negated all systems of defense because the expert jump shooter can get his shot away even when closely guarded and still make the basket. This does not infer that players should ignore considerations of defense and instead concentrate solely upon shooting techniques and aspects of attacking play. On the contrary, it is essential that all players should be well versed in the fundamentals of individual and team defensive methods in order that they make their opponents' task as difficult as possible. It follows that with teams of equal strength in attack, the team with the better defensive ability should always emerge as winners.

To most players, defensive play is not as exciting or as rewarding as attacking play. After all, the team on defense does not have possession of the ball and therefore is not using any of the individual handling skills which are the main source of pleasure and satisfaction of the game. It is, therefore, the duty of every coach to impress upon his players the importance of good defense to the team effort as a whole so that they regard it as a challenge to their ability and work as enthusiastically at considerations of defense as they do at those of attack. While the result of every game may well be determined by relative shooting efficiency this can be substantially influenced by the defensive methods employed. A team well drilled in defensive fundamentals can always provide the most effective counter to any system of attack, thus preventing their opponents from dictating the pattern of play and having an easy passage to baskets. A strong defense extends the opponents to the full and forces them to work hard, and think hard, for every point; a weak defense allows the opponents to utilize their talents to the best advantage and collect points at will.

It has already been asserted that basketball is in every sense a team game and nowhere is this more evident than in defensive play. The team defense can only be as strong as the individual defensive ability of its players. Whatever system of defense is being used, it will fall down if any one player is unable to safeguard its application. Experienced opponents can always adapt their attacking play to exploit any weakness in the opposing defense. There is no place in basketball for the player who considers his only function is to score baskets while the responsibility of defense rests with his teammates. No matter how many baskets he may score he must still fulfil his obligations in the team defense.

The demands upon the player when on defense, both physical and mental, are far greater than those in attacking play for on no account can he relax his efforts. If he must undergo a temporary phase of recovery while on court it should be done when his team is in possession and not when it is on defense. In attack, most moves revolve around two- or three-man plays, but in defense all players have an immediate responsibility that lasts until possession of the ball has been regained.

SYSTEMS OF DEFENSE

The two fundamental systems of defense used in basketball are Man-to-Man and Zone , though there are numerous variations and combinations of each. With beginners it should be considered obligatory for them to master the essentials of playing a basic man-to-man defense before even considering the introduction of any type of zone defense. Man-to-man defense teaches the fundamental principles that are required for the successful application of every type of defense.

MAN-TO-MAN DEFENSE—INDIVIDUAL

In the basic form of this defense each player in the team is responsible for one player in the opposing team and it is his duty to guard this player and this player only. Quite often this principle in itself is difficult for the beginner to grasp as invariably he will want to follow the ball wherever it goes. However, once he can be persuaded that two or more players converging on the one opponent with the ball must leave someone completely unguarded, he will begin to realize that the man-to-man system can only succeed if each player fulfils his own obligations and assumes his teammates will do likewise. Having been assigned this one opponent the player must do his utmost to prevent him from scoring and, as far as possible, play him out of the game by forcing him into errors or forestalling his intentions. In effect it is a battle of wits, one against the other, in which the defensive player tries to dominate his opponent.

Defensive Stance

(Diagram 26)

In the defensive stance the player must be well balanced with the weight distributed over both feet, which are spread comfortably apart with one foot in front of the other, and with the knees and hips slightly bent (Diagram 26). From this position of readiness, which resembles the boxer's or wrestler's stance, the defender can advance, retreat or move sideways in response to the need shown. Movement is made by sliding one foot at a time in the direction required, as in the boxer's shuffle, so that the legs are never crossed and the feet remain at least hip width apart. By sliding the feet in this way the player will never be

caught off balance but will be able to alter his direction of movement instantly should his opponent attempt a fake or suddenly
alter his line of progress. However, if the opponent succeeds in
breaking free, the defender should forsake this principle and turn
and run with him in order to resume a good defensive position.

DIAGRAM 26

The arms play an important role in the defensive stance with
one hand raised forward to discourage the shot or high pass and
the other one out to the side ready to interfere with an attempted
dribble or low pass. The alert defender will keep the arms
moving, interchanging them if necessary, according to the
immediate danger or in an attempt to influence the direction of
the play to his own team's advantage.

Floor Position

As a general rule, the defensive player should maintain a position
on the court so that he is directly in line with, and between, his
opponent and the basket. If the beginner regards this as the
golden rule of man-to-man defense he will not go far wrong.
Later, as his play develops, he will learn to modify this interpretation in order to have greater awareness of the play around
the ball and to use a better defense in certain situations.

The distance between the defensive player and his respective
opponent depends firstly upon the attacker's proximity to the

basket and secondly upon whether or not he is in possession. If the opponent is well out of shooting range he does not present an immediate threat and the defender can give him more latitude, merely keeping him in view and maintaining a position between him and the basket. As the opponent approaches shooting range the defender must move in to guard him more closely and the nearer he is to the basket the tighter and more aggressive should be the guarding.

When moving in to guard a man in the shooting area who is not in possession the defender should approach him quite slowly and not go in too close. If he is guarded too closely it gives him the opportunity to cut past the defender and receive a pass in the open because he always has that half a yard advantage. He knows when he is going to break but the defender does not! By keeping a yard or so away from his opponent the defender will not be caught in this way but always will be near enough to move in closer should the opponent receive the ball. Even when the player does receive the ball, or dribbles into shooting range with it, the defender should never rush right up to him but should take up his defensive stance about arm's length away. Apart from the danger of committing a foul, the closer a defender is to his attacking opponent the easier it is for the opponent to get past him and this is a very real danger if the opponent has not used up his dribble.

Guarding the Dribbler

There are different schools of thought as to which are the best defensive tactics to be adopted when opposed by an attacking dribbler. What most coaches do agree upon is that the defender should concentrate upon playing the opponent rather than stealing the ball; if he can be robbed of possession as well, then so much the better.

The divergence of opinion regarding the best tactics to counter the dribbler typifies basketball tactics in general. At one time many of the leading coaches advocated that the dribbler should be forced to the side line because, they argued, a player is least effective from this position either as a scoring threat or for setting up plays. This policy was, therefore, adopted by the majority of teams. Then, at a later date, some coaches put forward the theory that it was better to force the dribbler towards the center because a team's defensive strength is usually greatest along this line. This policy is directly opposed to the other one, yet, on the surface, it appears equally sound. Obviously, it is wrong to make sweeping generalizations with regard to these or any other tactics of the game and defenders must take the action that is most appropriate for the particular situation, player and overall team strategy. What may prove most effective in one instance may be utterly wrong in another. For example, if the attacking dribbler has shown himself to have a very strong driving side, the defender may choose to force him in the opposite direction regardless of whether it is towards the side line or the center.

Once the defender has assumed the best possible defensive position between the dribbler and the basket and succeeded in forestalling the intended line of attack, he may then consider stealing the ball if the opponent persists in dribbling it. This is best achieved by trying to tap the ball upwards at a point near the floor because the dribbler has least control here and there is less chance of committing a personal foul. However, when attempting to steal the ball the defender must not be careless regarding his fundamental defensive movements otherwise the attacker may elude him by means of a sudden change of pace or direction and get past him after all.

When opposed by a fast breaking attack the defender may find himself fundamentally out of position in that he is not between the dribbler and the basket; he may even be behind the dribbler! In these circumstances the defender must do his utmost to get ahead of the dribbler in order to gain a good defensive position and he can only hope to do this if he forgets about the ball and goes all out for the floor position.

At all times the good defender will concentrate on the dribbler first and the ball second!

Guarding the Shooter

One objective of all defensive play is to force the opponents to make their scoring attempts under the most unfavourable conditions possible. The ultimate objective is, of course, to prevent them from scoring at all and there should always be an attempt at blocking the shot when it is eventually taken. The more thorough is the guard in his defensive stance and positioning, the better able he will be to reach up and block the shot when it is attempted by his opponent. Blocking calls for good anticipation and timing so that a defender makes his effort at the correct moment in order to jump high and reach over the ball with the outstretched hand. If the jump is too late the shooter will get the ball away as intended; if the jump is too soon the attacker may change his mind and dribble past the guard while he is in the air or take the shot as the guard returns to the ground. Once a defender has left the floor he cannot change his mind! He is helpless until gravity has brought him back into contact with the floor.

When guarding the shooter the defender must not commit himself unless a shot is really being taken; but when it is being taken he must make an all-out effort to get up and block the shot.

Guarding the Out-of-Bounds Player

No special tactics are needed to guard an out-of-bounds player if the ball is being brought in from a position well outside the scoring area; the normal principles hold good. It is another matter if the ball is being brought into play near or within the danger area and easy points are offered to the opponents if the defenders do not know how to cope with this situation. The pertinent factor regarding this situation is that the out-of-bounds player is not an immediate threat because he is not permitted to shoot. The defender guarding him, therefore, should not move in close and face him as is customary but should drop back and stand sideways so that he can watch his opponent and the other players around the ball. By these tactics he can, if necessary, assist in picking up an attacking player who breaks free but he is still in contact with his own opponent should the ball be returned to him. If he guarded his opponent in the normal way he would have his back to the play and would give his opponents the opportunity of an easy screen play.

Guarding the Pivot Player

(Diagram 27)

Although the fundamental guarding position is directly between the player and the basket, guarding the pivot player is an instance where this principle may be completely reversed, particularly if the pivot player in question is a very tall man and the key player of the opponents' attack.

Normally, the pivot player takes up a position with his back

to the basket immediately outside the free-throw lane or on the free-throw line. If he is an accomplished specialist in the hook or turn-around shots it is not sufficient for the defender to stand between him and the basket, for on receiving the ball he will still be able to get his shot away and the defender will be unable to block it. When guarding such a specialist the defender should do his utmost to prevent him from receiving the ball at all and must position himself accordingly. If the pivot player is on the free-throw line the defender will stand behind him but slightly offset to one side, corresponding to the location of the ball, with the arm that is nearer to the ball outstretched so

DIAGRAM 27

that incoming passes are discouraged. If the play switches to the other side of the court the defender will stand at the other side of the pivot player with that arm outstretched. Similarly, if the pivot player takes up a position outside the free-throw lane the defender will stand alongside him with the arm outstretched so that once again it is between the ball and the pivot player, but so that he is still in a position to cut off the pivot player's direct approach to the basket. In extreme cases where the pivot player stations himself outside the free-throw lane near to the end line, or is moving across the free-throw lane close to the basket, the defender may actually keep in front of the pivot player, as this will be the surest way of preventing him from getting the ball.

Guarding the good pivot player is an especially difficult proposition and one that calls for intelligent defensive measures on the part of the guard. It is largely a matter of experience combined with sound defensive ability so that the defender knows just when, and by how much, to overshift in order to prevent the incoming pass, yet at the same time not give the pivot player the chance to cut past him and receive a pass in the open for an easy basket. The task of guarding the pivot player should be assigned to an alert and aggressive defender.

Guarding when Outnumbered

In any system of defense it is important that all players be strategically placed as soon as possible after possession has been lost, in order that the opponents do not set up their attack with a numerical superiority. Man-to-man defense relies upon each player's accounting for one opponent; if at any time the attack outnumbers the defense it means that there must always be someone who is unguarded.

Whenever this situation arises and a defender is confronted by two or more opponents in the dangerous shooting area and his team-mates are out of position, he must forget his fundamental man-to-man principles and have as his objective the protection of the area under the basket. On no account must he let any of the attackers have open running space for a close shot at the basket. He should try to delay the attackers so that his team-mates can recover their defensive positions or at least force the shot to be attempted from somewhere outside the close shooting area, so that there is more chance of the basket being missed. The defender can best achieve this by challenging, or by faking a challenge, at whomever has the ball, at the same time keeping in contact with the frontal attacker, so that his path to the basket can always be blocked.

Defensive Rebounding

The team that controls the backboards is the team that controls the game. This is a well-worn basketball phrase but like many such phrases it has more than an element of truth. Certainly no team should underestimate the consequences of rebounding on the game. If a defending team consistently fails to secure the rebounds from its own backboard it means that the opponents are given a further opportunity to make good the missed shots instead of losing possession.

Whenever an attacker has succeeded in getting a shot away while reasonably close to the basket, the defender's immediate aim should be to block out his opponent's path to the basket so that he cannot establish a good rebounding position. As soon as the shot has been launched the defender must not turn his head or body to watch the flight of the ball, otherwise he will momentarily lose contact with his opponent and let him through for the rebound. Instead, he should take a step back and continue to face his opponent. When the attacker follows up his shot the defender can then move in front of him to cut off the direct path to the basket and take up a stance facing squarely toward the basket just a few feet away from it, ready to collect the rebound. In this stance the defender has his feet spread and the knees slightly bent in readiness for the jump; the head is up watching the ball. As with so many other skills in basketball, good rebounding depends largely upon correct timing. The defender must judge his jump so that he takes the ball in both hands at the peak of his jump with the body at full stretch. It is bad policy to tap the ball when rebounding in an attempt to thwart an opponent; as often as not the ball will go to one or other of the opponents and present him with an easy shot at the basket. If a defender is sufficiently well placed to tap the ball then he should be able to grasp it. On collecting the ball the defender must not instinctively take it down low but should be prepared to keep it high and throw a quick pass to a teammate who is well placed to initiate a fast break. At other times he can bring the ball down for protection before making the first pass, or dribble to another position on the floor as a prelude to setting up an attacking play.

MAN-TO-MAN DEFENSE — TEAM

No matter how expert players may become in their individual defensive skills it will be of little use if they are not co-ordinated into a unified team defense. Ability to adapt and apply the team defense to combat the particular opponents and the ensuing game situations is as vital as sound fundamentals.

Player Assignment

Many reputable coaches go to extreme lengths to arrive at the best solution when allocating man-to-man duties, even to the extent of sending out scouts to make a detailed analysis of the forthcoming opponents so that they can plan the defensive measures accordingly. However, some coaches are reluctant to take tactics as seriously as this but it is obviously in the interests of a team to match up its players in an effort to minimize the opponents' attacking strength, rather than just trust to luck. In the basic form of man-to-man defense each player is responsible for one opponent and one opponent only, therefore it would be defensively unsound to put a small player against a tall player who possesses accurate overhead shooting ability, nor would it be wise to match the weakest defender against the star of the opposing team. The coach should always try to deploy his players to provide the most effective defense against the opponents in question. At most levels of basketball it is sufficient to match up defenders on the basis of height, speed and shooting ability of the opponents so that no undue advantage is gained in any of these quarters.

For basic man-to-man defense to be successful each player must always know the identity of the opponent he is guarding. At the start of the game this is simple enough as the coach can allocate guard duties in advance, upon the basis just mentioned, as soon as he knows the opposing team's opening line-up. However, as the game progresses substitutions may occur on both sides and new players brought into the game. When such alterations are made the coach or captain must ensure that there is no misunderstanding regarding allocation of responsibility, so that the moment play is resumed each defender is fully aware of his own assigned player. If doubt exists, the opposing team may be presented with an easy basket because one of its players is unguarded.

An alternative method of player assignment that is favored by some coaches when teams are fairly evenly matched is the one in which the players do not have a previously defined opponent to guard but select their man as each separate attack develops. In this system the defenders pick up their respective opponents according to their position on the court when possession was lost. The player nearest the defensive basket will guard the frontal attacker, his closest colleague will take the next most dangerous attacker and so on. This method of player assignment is not recommended for beginners as it may lead to confusion, with players not knowing soon enough the opponent for whom they are responsible. Experienced players are able to make a quick decision and assessment of the situation and select their appropriate opponent before the attack can establish any threat to the basket. Even so, there must be complete understanding among the players.

Switching Man-to-Man Defense

In the basic interpretation of man-to-man defense each player has one opponent to guard and is responsible for guarding only this player until possession has been regained by his own team. The identity of his opponent may change from time to time during the course of the game, due to substitution or alteration in player assignment by the coach to improve the team defense, but in any one attack the defender knows he must stick to just one player. This straightforward application of man-to-man defense is adequate when learning the game but as the standard of play develops it may not necessarily be the best tactics to cope with the attacking play of the opposing team.

The principal weakness of man-to-man defense is its susceptibility to screen play (see next chapter on Principles of Attack) in which the defender is made to lose contact with his opponent due to a temporary obstruction dividing him from his man. When this occurs the attacker is able to break free from his guard. One method of countering screen play is for the team to employ a switching man-to-man defense in which players exchange assignments as the screen is set up in order to prevent one man from getting free. In Diagram 28(a) defender A will lose contact with his opponent, attacker 1, at the moment this player passes close to his teammate number 2 because A's path will be blocked by player 2 and his own teammate B who is guarding this player. By employing a switch of assignments as this occurs, defender B going with number 1 and defender A changing to player 2, the defenders will forestall the screen and prevent number 1 from breaking free (Diagram 28(b)).

When using this system of man-to-man defense it is of paramount importance that players have a complete understanding with each other and are well drilled in employing the switch at the critical moment. If there is any doubt or hesitation in applying the switch the defenders will probably give the attackers a better opportunity to get one man free than they would have achieved from the screen! The defenders must not be afraid to talk to each other, one player warning his team-mate of a probable switch of assignments, so that both are pre-pared should the screen be attempted. Manual assistance can also be of value in making a good switch, one player pushing or pulling his colleague at the critical moment. The onus for these decisions should normally be taken by the defender nearer to the basket as he is better placed to assess the situation.

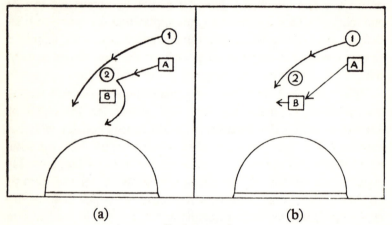

(a)   (b)

DIAGRAM 28

The danger in using a switching man-to-man defense is for players to switch assignments unnecessarily. Indiscriminate switching often leads to a deterioration in carrying out individual defensive duties because players tend to lose sight of the fact that they are, after all, responsible for guarding one particular opponent. The switch should only be employed if the intended screen will enable the opponents to gain a dangerous advantage. On many occasions there may be no real problem posed by being temporarily blocked out from the opponent and it may be possible to restore a good defensive position before any threat can be established. At other times defenders may be able to get through the screen quite easily without committing a foul. In such circumstances a switch is not justified. Only experience will enable the players to determine when a switch should be employed, hence it is not a system that should be introduced until players are fully conversant with basic man-to-man defense.

Sagging Man-to-Man Defense

Another inherent disadvantage of the basic man-to-man defense is the excessive demands it places upon stamina. If a defender pursues his opponent continually whenever the other team is in possession he will soon become exhausted and be unable to fulfil his defensive obligations to good effect. To reduce the expenditure on physical effort a team can employ a sagging man-to-man defense in which the players away from the ball guard their man very loosely and sag toward the basket area. The defender guarding the ball handler, however, observes strict man-to-man principles. In this variation of man-to-man defense the defenders not immediately concerned with the play are concentrated in the important scoring area instead of following their opponents closely wherever they go. A sagging man-to-man defense also helps to eliminate susceptibility to screen plays because obstructions can only be set up when close man-to-man guarding is being used.

A sagging man-to-man defense gives the appearance of a zone defense because the players are concentrated around the basket; some of them may even be well away from their opponents. Nevertheless, it must be remembered that this type of defense is still man-to-man and players must adopt this role strictly as soon as their particular opponent receives the ball or cuts towards the ball handler. The emphasis with a sagging man-to-man defense is to deny the opponents a ready path to the basket by congesting the area around the basket. Obviously it is not a maneuver to be used against a team that has strong outside shooters.

Pressing Man-to-Man Defense

Sagging man-to-man defense is one extreme of the basic interpretation and pressing man-to-man is the other. It is so strenuous to apply that it is not commonly adopted as a system of defense for the whole game but more as a form of tactics to be used for a limited period in order to upset the rhythm of the opponents' attack. As a means to this end, pressing man-to-man can prove most effective.

When playing the pressing system defenders guard their respective opponents on strict man-to-man principles no matter where they move on the court and regardless of whether or not they have the ball. If a full court press is being used the defenders commence this aggressive guarding the moment possession of the ball changes to the opponents. Each player immediately picks up his opponent and sticks to him like glue! If a half court press is being used then the defenders adopt these same tactics as soon as their opponents have passed the half-way mark. The idea of the press is for the defenders to guard their opponents closely wherever they may go so that they are forced into errors or violations and so that it is made extremely difficult for them to give or receive passes. Pressing man-to-man defense demands that players are superbly fit, sound in techniques of man-to-man guarding and able to hustle opponents without committing fouls.

Defending the Fast-Break Attack

The simplest and most effective form of attack, if allowed to function, is the fast break. As the name implies, the fast break relies upon a team establishing its pattern of attack before the opponents have had time to set up their defense. If a fast break is successfully launched the attackers will outnumber the defenders when the ball reaches the scoring area.

The critical point of the fast break is the first pass after possession has changed from one team to the other, for it is at this moment that a team may be least strategically placed to apply correct defensive measures. To combat the fast-break attack the defenders should try to stall the first pass and so gain time to set up the team defense. Possession normally changes hands after a shot has been made and if follow-up tactics are used by at least two players it will be possible for the opposing ball handler to be closely pressed the moment he gains possession of the ball thus delaying the first pass and allowing the defenders to retreat to sound defensive positions. As often as not when using the fast break a team will persist with a stereotyped method of initiating the attack and it may be possible for the defenders to give further discouragement to the opponents if, on losing possession, another defender immediately presses the player who normally receives the first pass. Pressing tactics upon the key men the moment possession is lost is the best defense against a team that favors the fast-break attack.

However, if a fast break attack has been set in motion and the defenders find themselves outnumbered they must concentrate on protecting the under-basket area so that the attackers are not allowed easy access to make a close shot. In most instances it will be two defenders against three attackers, in which case the forward defender must challenge the ball handler while his colleague drops back towards the basket. As the ball is switched from one attacker to another the nearer defender must move in to challenge the new handler while the other takes responsibility for the under-basket area. These tactics will not only close the direct path to the basket but will also help to slow up the attack giving the other defenders time to get back and assist their outnumbered colleagues, picking up opponents in order of priority.

ZONE DEFENSE

For a long time teams in this country persisted in using zone methods of defense almost exclusively, and even now many teams still cling rigidly to this system regardless of the situation. Undoubtedly zone defense has many virtues to commend it but it has been used by teams not because it is the best method but because of an inability to apply sound man-to-man defense. The zone method has been the easier solution to the problems of defense. Good man-to-man defense requires sustained physical and mental application and a thorough knowledge of the fundamentals of individual guarding. Players in this country have shirked the hard work necessary to master these fundamentals and have thankfully grasped at the zone method to meet all situations. Two domestic factors have further encouraged, and to a certain extent justified, this preference for zone methods. In the first instance the majority of basketball in this country is played on small courts and secondly the general standard of outside shooting is lamentably behind that of the rest of the basketball world; given these conditions zone methods are reasonably adequate to cope with most situations.

ZONE DEFENSE—INDIVIDUAL

The various techniques of individual guarding as described in man-to-man defense apply no less in zone defense; it is merely that the defenders concentrate upon the location of the ball instead of a particular opponent. Each player is assigned a specific area of the court to defend and whenever the ball is in his territory he must guard the ball handler, whoever he may be, on strict man-to-man principles. When the ball is not in his own territory the guard must continue to face it and shift about the floor, within the limits of his defined area, in order to support his teammates.

Zone defense is not static; the defenders continually adjust their floor position in relation to the whereabouts of the ball. As the ball moves about the court each defender will shift to the part of his own zone that is nearest to the ball while still keeping in contact with any attacker in his area. The actual shape and size of each defender's own area of responsibility will depend upon the type of zone being used by the team. As a general rule it can be regarded as a circle but this may flatten or elongate in order to conform to the team defense (see Diagram 29). There must, of course, be a certain amount of overlap between the areas of the five defenders so that all the danger area is covered and there are no gaps left that will allow the attackers a path through to the basket.

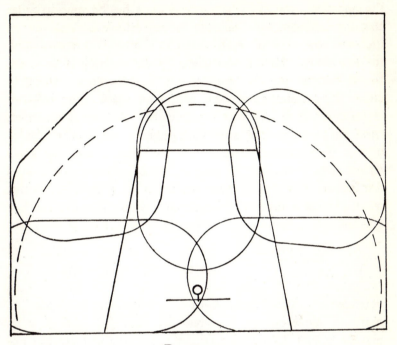

DIAGRAM 29

ZONE DEFENSE—TEAM

The idea behind zone defense is for the team to divide up the dangerous scoring territory between its five players so that there is always someone strategically placed to deal with a shooting attempt and all scoring lanes to the basket can be blocked. By virtue of the fact that each defender's territory of operation is restricted to a defined area it follows that zone defense is less exhausting to play than man-to-man defense. Also, as there is not as much movement and close guarding in this type of defense, it is far less vulnerable to driving and screen plays.

Opposed to these advantages, however, is the fact that no zone defense can provide an answer to a team that possesses good outside shooters. The better the outside shooting ability of the opponents the more widespread must be the zone in order that the defenders can challenge the ball handlers. This in turn increases the size of each defender's area of responsibility, making his task harder, and opens up the shooting lanes to the basket because players have too far to shift when moving to cover the extremities of their own floor space. The ball can travel far more quickly than the defender! As already indicated, these problems do not arise when playing on small courts or against poor shooters because the zone has a relatively small danger area to account for and so can be concentrated around the basket. Any type of zone defense is weak on a large court when playing a team of good shooters who can move the ball quickly.

Another weakness of zone methods is its vulnerability to double teaming tactics. Against a zone defense the attackers can outnumber the defenders at any given point because each defender is restricted to a defined area of the court and, normally, must not move outside this area. By placing a number of its players in one defender's territory the attacking team can put pressure on the zone at that point; if the other defenders shift beyond the limits of their own territory to support their outnumbered colleague the zone will be weakened elsewhere and scoring lanes opened up.

There are numerous basic team formations of zone defense that can be adopted in order to divide up the danger area between the five defenders and each one has its particular strengths and weaknesses. No matter which formation is being used by a team it is essential that players retreat quickly after losing possession in order to set up the zone before the opponents have established their attack otherwise the team defense will be non-existent.

Three-Two Zone

The three-two formation, in which there are three players in the front line of defense and two in the rear, was probably the first method of zone defense to be used and is still very popular with many teams, especially those that favour the fast break as their own method of attack. This formation enables them to have three men well up in attack as soon as possession has been gained. Despite its popularity this zone system is fundamentally weak as the center of the zone is not adequately covered and this usually results in the two rear men being drawn too far from the basket in order to block out the center.

Two-One-Two Zone

This formation is a logical variation of the previous one in that the center man of the front line drops back to cover the central area. The two-one-two type of zone is the one most frequently used by teams that prefer zone methods and it is quite effective against teams that rely on a good pivot player as the source of most of their baskets; it also gives a strong defense round the backboard for taking rebounds because the center player can complete a defensive triangle to block out the attackers. The main weakness of the two-one-two formation is at the sides of the zone because all the defenders tend to be drawn into the center making the total coverage of the zone relatively small. However, as a general purpose zone it is undoubtedly the most effective formation against most forms of attack, especially if the two front men and the center man have good understanding and can co-ordinate their chasing.

One-Two-Two Zone

Of the more usual formations the one-two-two is probably the easiest to play and the most difficult for the opponents to penetrate, but it is completely ineffective against a team that possesses even moderate outside shooting ability. By having one man well forward the defense can often force the opposing team to commit itself early but the zone itself has a very small defensive coverage because the front man contributes little to the actual defense once the ball has reached the effective shooting range.

Practically any combination of five men can be chosen for the basic pattern of the defense (one-three-one and two-three zones are just two others that are frequently used) though once in operation against the attack it is often hard to distinguish which zone is being used because the players are constantly shifting their positions within their defined territory in order to support their colleagues. When selecting the starting formation, however, the team should use the line-up that will give them the strongest defense to combat the opponents' method of attack. If the opponents rely on a strong pivot player then the two-one-two will probably be the best zone, whereas if they possess players who prefer to drive in close to the basket, a two-three zone may provide the answer. It is wrong for teams to stick rigidly to one type of zone regardless of the situation; they must be able to suit the zone to combat the opponents' tactics.

COMBINATION DEFENSES

No one defensive system, whether zone or man-to-man, can possibly supply the complete answer to all the problems of defense. In many instances a combination defense in which certain features of both are co-ordinated into one system will provide the solution to a particular situation. Needless to say, teams must be competent in the fundamental application of both man-to-man and zone defenses before they can aspire to combination defenses.

Triangle and Two

In this defense two men play on a strict man-to-man basis while their three colleagues play a triangular zone round the basket.

The triangle and two defense can be used to good effect against a team that relies on one or two expert ball handlers feeding the ball to a strong pivot player. The two men playing on a man-to-man basis try to prevent the ball handlers from setting up the play and getting the ball to the pivot player while the triangle defends the basket area with one of them always blocking out the pivot player depending on whose territory he is in.

Box and Dog

The box and dog defense has long been a favorite system against a team that depends upon the passing or shooting prowess of just one key player. One defender, the dog, assumes the responsibility of playing the star man right out of the game by marking him continually on strict man-to-man principles. The remaining defenders play a four-man zone in a two-two formation.

Diamond and Dog

This combination defense is merely a variation of the previous one. The dog still guards the star player on a strict man-to-man basis but the four defenders playing the zone take up a one-two-one formation in front of the basket. By playing the zone this way the team has a stronger defense against shots from the side than in the box zone but is weaker under the basket because there is only one defender in the back line.

These three systems are the most commonly used of the combination defenses and are typical of the way in which certain advantages of man-to-man and zone methods can be brought together to provide the best defense to meet the particular circumstances. The problems of defense are seldom a straightforward matter of whether to use man-to-man or zone; they are a challenge to the team to arrive at the right compromise of the various defensive principles and this can only be founded upon sound knowledge of the two basic systems.

DEFENSIVE DRILLS

Just as drills can help players become proficient in the handling skills so also can they assist in developing good defensive ability. Once the players have learned the essentials of defensive work it is largely a matter of building up experience and this process can be accelerated through practice of defensive drills. Players may not find these as interesting as many of the other practices but they are invaluable to the coach for improving the individual and team defense of his players.

1. One-on-One Drill

One player with a ball takes up a position by the half way mark and acts as an attacker; his partner assumes a defensive stance between him and the basket. The attacker attempts to dribble the ball in for a lay-up or other close shot while the defender guards him on strict man-to-man basis and tries to prevent the shot or force the attacker to commit himself before he reaches close shooting range.

This is a fundamental guarding drill for man-to-man defense and the coach must watch carefully for any errors or weaknesses in the defensive measures taken by his players and give constant correction so that good habits are formed.

2. Zone-Shifting Drill

Five players take up zone positions in any one of the set formations as decreed by the coach. Some eight to twelve players form up in a semi-circle around the outside of the zone. The ball is interpassed rapidly by the outnumbering attacking players, not necessarily in any set sequence, and the defensive players must constantly shift their positions so that the zone is always covering the threat of the ball handler in accordance with zone principles. No attempt at shooting is made in this drill.

This is a fundamental guarding drill for zone defense and

the coach should take up a good observation position so that he can criticize the maneuvering of the defenders and stop the drill as and when desirable to give coaching and corrections. It is a strenuous drill for the defenders and the players should be changed frequently.

3. Screen-Switch Drill

(Diagram 30)

Some six or eight players form up in two files of attackers and defenders as shown in Diagram 30. Players 1 and 4 cut across

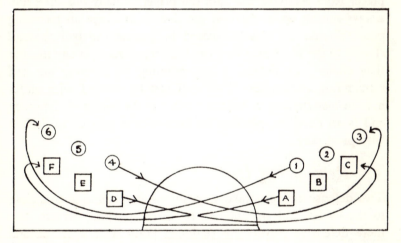

DIAGRAM 30

the court with their respective defenders, A and D, moving with them on man-to-man guarding principles. As the attackers cross, the defenders must switch opponents and take over guarding duties on the other attacker. Each player joins the end of the opposite line and the same drill is continued by the next four players. Attacking and guarding duties are changed over from time to time so that everyone gets practice at switching. No ball is required.

Once again the coach must stand at a good observation point and criticize the movements of the defenders. In particular he must make sure that the defenders switch at the correct instant and that they assist each other in making the switch.

4. Pivot-Defense Drill

Four attacking players are positioned in a semi-circle around five defenders and are allowed to pass the ball freely around the perimeter while seeking the opportunity of getting a pass through to a pivot player who is free to move across the free throw lane anywhere between the basket and the free-throw line.

The defenders must do their utmost to prevent the pivot player from receiving the ball, the player actually guarding him always setting up in the best position to intercept an incoming pass. Should the attack succeed in getting the ball through cleanly to the pivot man they can then try to score in any manner they choose, the defenders concentrating on blocking out and rebounding techniques. This drill can be worked with either man-to-man defense or zone according to the wishes of the coach and is an excellent practice for accustoming players to dealing with pivot play.

5. Rebounding Drill

Two defensive players take up positions as rebound guards close to the basket and are opposed by three attacking players; two more defensive players are stationed fairly wide apart beyond the free-throw line. The coach stands on the free-throw line and tosses the ball at the ring or backboard so that it rebounds into play. The defensive players endeavor to block out the attackers, secure the rebound and pass immediately to one of their forward teammates. The attacking players must try to get through the block and take the rebound. Positions are changed frequently and the coach watches for any faults or weaknesses in rebounding technique.

5 *Principles of Attack*

THE TEAM in possession of the ball is the attacking team and it remains so until a basket is scored or possession is gained by the opponents. Regardless of the team tactics employed the final analysis of success will always be directly related to the individual player's grasp of the basic techniques. Every system of attack must be built upon sound fundamentals and training and practice should be devoted exclusively to this aspect long before consideration is given to team methods of attack. Even when the stage is reached that players are sufficiently proficient and the coach can concentrate on the wider implications of the game, the practice of pure fundamentals must never be discarded but still allocated a proportion of every training session.

The main fundamental techniques and skills of attacking play have already been discussed in detail in the earlier chapters on individual skills. It is the combined application of these various handling and movement skills that provide the team attack. Unless each player has mastered these techniques and knows how best to use them his contribution to the team attack will be seriously restricted, especially if he is up against good defensive players. As in defensive work, the best application of attacking skills will depend largely upon the particular circumstances in any given game and should be dictated by the situations as they arise. In this respect, players should study closely the defensive tactics of the opponents as a team and their defensive skill and ability as individuals. By discovering any weaknesses and adjusting the attacking play accordingly it will be possible to set up scoring opportunities that might otherwise not present themselves. Nearly every attack on the basket is the culmination of a two or three man play but all five players must regard themselves as attackers every time their team has possession of the ball so that the opponents' defense is extended to the full. If each individual player is a potential threat, both as a scorer and as a play maker , the opponents cannot neglect guarding duties on any one member of the team in order to team up on key players. Although most attacks do stem from two and three man plays and although most teams do have one or two players who score the majority of points, attacking play is very much a matter of team effort; and, as with defensive work, the team effort is dependent upon the attacking ability of the individual players.

ATTACKING PLAY—INDIVIDUAL

Triple-Threat Position
(Diagram 31)

The initiative in basketball is always with the attacker for he

has the advantage in that he knows his own intentions a split second before they become apparent to the defender. The good player exploits this advantage by constantly disguising his intentions, thus making the defender's task even more difficult; if intentions are telegraphed to the guard he is better prepared to counter the forthcoming threat.

An important aid in helping to retain maximum initiative is the use of the triple-threat position by the ball handler on receiving a pass when within shooting range. If the pass is not to be followed by an immediate attacking action the player should balance the ball in a comfortable shooting position in front of the chest, with one foot in front of the other and the

DIAGRAM 31

body perfectly balanced and poised for action. From this position the player can just as easily shoot for the basket, commence a dribble or pass to a teammate, and neither his stance nor the ball's position will betray to the guard which tactic is to be employed. This triple-threat position means that the guard must be prepared to counter all of these actions, thus making his task extremely difficult and putting him at a marked disadvantage. Those attackers who indicate their intentions in advance, or those who partially commit themselves by instinctively bouncing the ball on the floor as soon as they receive it, reduce their attacking potential and make the defenders' task far easier. The player who uses up his dribble by instinctively bouncing the ball when he receives it throws away one of his three privileges as an attacker and his opponent can immediately move in to discourage the shot or pass. The defender who moves in close to a triple-threat attacker may find the attacker has dribbled past him before he can take correct defensive measures.

Feint and Shot

(Diagram 32)

Feinting and faking are vital tactics of attacking play and are complementary to sound fundamental techniques. When opposed by a good defensive player the attacker must use these ruses to disguise his intentions even further and to put the guard off balance.

The feint and shot can be used in the shooting territory against a defender who tends to guard too closely. Starting from the triple-threat position, the attacker lunges forward with one foot and the ball as though commencing a dribble. This action should cause the defender to step back in order to cover the threatened drive. As soon as the guard has committed himself by moving backwards the attacker returns quickly to the shooting position and takes an uninterrupted shot at the basket. At no time does the grip on the ball alter, thus enabling the player to make the shot with the minimum of delay or, should he so choose, throw a pass or commence a dribble if the response of the guard makes one of these other actions preferable.

DIAGRAM 32

Fake and Drive

(Diagram 33)

From the same all-important triple-threat position the attacker lunges to the side with one foot, moving his head and shoulders and the ball also, as though commencing a dribble in that

DIAGRAM 33

direction. As the guard shifts to cover the threatened drive, the attacker brings the foot back, executes a long cross-over step in the other direction and commences a dribble and drive round the guard who has opened up a lane by committing himself in the wrong direction. It is essential that a deep cross-over step is made as soon as the guard reacts to the fake so that the ball is protected by the body and leg as the dribble is started and the attacker can drive past the guard before he can recover sufficiently to cut off the intended path. The hand furthest away from the guard will be the one used to commence the dribble.

Up-and-Under Drive

(Diagram 34)

This tactic of attack is similar in principle to the previous one except that the dribble and drive are preceded by a fake shot at

DIAGRAM 34

the basket. The attacker holds the ball in front of the chest, in the normal triple-threat position, and gets set as though making a shooting attempt at the basket in order to tempt the guard to come in close to block the supposed shot. The fake is made more complete if the attacker keeps his eyes trained on the basket, bends and straightens the knees and starts to bring the ball up in front of the face as at the commencement of a shot. If properly executed, this fake should cause the guard to rise up on his toes to block the anticipated shot or even to jump off the floor. As soon as the guard has committed himself the attacker takes a long stride forward and drives past the guard keeping low down so that the ball is afforded maximum protection. When making the initial stride the player should do so with the leg nearer to the guard on passing him so that it helps to cover the ball as it is dribbled with the opposite hand.

Cutting

Rapid starting and stopping, change of pace and direction, and the other techniques of footwork play a vital role in attacking play, for these are the maneuvers that must be used to outwit the defense and open up scoring opportunities. Basketball is essentially a dynamic game and players should cultivate the habit of being continually on the move when their side has possession of the ball so that the defense never knows from which quarter danger may suddenly threaten. It is not sufficient for players to move about the court in regular patterns or once again the defenders will be able to anticipate any threat. In addition to the previously mentioned techniques of footwork, players should develop good cutting ability so that they can decide when and how to break from their guard to get free for a pass.

Many players show a natural aptitude for this phase of the game and always seem to be in the right place at the right time; with others it is more a matter of developing this facility through experience. As a general rule the purpose of most cutting movements is for the player to get free of his guard so that he can take the ball on the run and either drive in to the basket for a close shot or set up a play for one of his team-mates. One of the most effective methods of cutting is the angle cut in which the player runs down the side of the court, or diagonally across it, in the general direction of one corner and then by employing a sudden change of direction cuts hard across the open basket area to receive a lead pass, usually from the opposite direction. The essence of this cut, as indeed with all cutting movements, is good timing otherwise the cutter may arrive at the critical point a fraction of a second too soon to receive the pass and his guard will be able to catch up and counter the intended dribble and drive. If he arrives there too late the cut will be wasted effort because the opportunity for the pass will be lost. So that scoring lanes to the basket are left open for cutters it is important that the attacking players keep clear of this area while circling the court, otherwise it might become too congested for cutters to receive a pass.

Reverse and Drive

In this attacking play the player cuts quickly toward the ball handler and on receiving a pass stops suddenly, pivots sharply and then immediately drives back round his guard and dribbles in for the basket. Split-second timing is the keynote for this tactic so that the quick stop and pivot on receiving the ball is sufficient to give the attacker the vital half pace advantage necessary for him to get ahead of his guard to commence the dribble.

Jump-Ball Situations

With the elimination of a jump ball after every basket this game situation no longer assumes the importance it once held. Indeed, at one time the course of a game could well be dictated by the outcome of the jump-ball situations because they often enabled one team to monopolize possession if it was fortunate enough to have an outstanding jump-ball exponent. Even so, all players in the team may still be concerned in jump-ball situations during the course of the game so it is a consideration that should not be overlooked. While it must be conceded that the taller player is at an advantage, good leaping ability and good timing are factors of paramount importance and these can be developed through practice. At a jump ball the referee must toss the ball above the effective jumping height of both players and as they are permitted to tap it only after it has started its descent, good judgment and jumping can often offset disparity in height between the two players concerned.

The normal technique adopted at a jump ball is for the player to stand sideways to his opponent with both feet close together and the knees partially bent so that the body is in a semi-crouch position of readiness. As the official tosses the ball into the air the eyes are focused on it and the explosive upward jump made so that the ball can be tapped with the fingertips at the peak of the jump with the arm and body fully extended. The player must also know in advance the teammate to whom he is attempting to pass and the point at which the ball will be received; this will be in accordance with the team strategy (see team considerations later). If unsuccessful at the jump ball the opponents become the attacking team so all players must immediately establish good defensive positions.

It is often forgotten, or sometimes not even known, that a second tap is permissible at a jump ball. The player should always be prepared to make use of this privilege should it prove necessary or advisable in the interests of securing possession.

Attacking Rebound Play

As already suggested, the team that controls the backboards controls the game, therefore good rebounding ability is an important consideration of attacking play. The attacking re-bounders are usually at a disadvantage because it is easier for the defenders to gain the inside position around the basket. This handicap is partially offset by the fact that the defensive guard is usually trying to secure the ball with both hands while the attacking rebounder is merely trying to tap the ball into the basket with the fingertips.

The technique of rebounding in attack, like jump-ball situations, is primarily a matter of good timing combined with good jumping ability. The object of the rebounder is to meet the ball at the peak of his upward jump, with the body and arms fully extended, after it has rebounded from the ring or backboard. As the fingertips make contact with the ball it is flicked into the basket, usually via the backboard, with a wrist and finger action. The effective jumping height of the rebounder is increased if he can use a one-handed tip-in shot but it is better to concentrate on the two-handed version until timing and control have been mastered. Any team that possesses good rebounders who can dominate the backboard in attack has a truly demoralizing weapon.

Screening

Screen play is apt to be something of a mystery to beginning players and is often regarded as merely a maneuver aimed at complicating what would otherwise be a simple game! Nothing could be further from the truth. Screen play in one form or another is a fundamental strategy of attacking basketball and is used by all teams when opposed by man-to-man defense even though sometimes it may not be intentional.

In its simplest interpretation, screen play is a tactic whereby the attacking team causes obstacles to be set up between one of its players and his guard so that the attacker is momentarily unguarded and can break free. A screen is most commonly set up when an attacker runs his guard into a stationary teammate (see Diagram 28(a), so that he himself can break away; alternatively, an attacking player can set up a screen by positioning himself next to an opponent so that his teammate guarded by this opponent can break free. Screen play can prove a most effective tactic against a close man-to-man defense because it enables an attacking player to get free in order to drive in to the basket or receive the ball for an uninterrupted shot. However, success is not necessarily assured simply because a team is able to set up screens; success depends upon the ability of the players to anticipate a possible screen and break away at the critical moment should it materialize.

Screen play is largely a matter of experience and it should be featured prominently in training sessions, players continually setting up screens for each other in two and three man plays so that they develop the ability to see potential screens and react immediately to these screens once they have been set up. The keynote of all screen plays should be simplicity and the coach should drill his players accordingly.

The potential attacking strength of any team can be no greater than that permitted by the technical ability of its individual players, and the team tactics should be styled to utilize their particular talents to the utmost. It is useless for a team to base its attack upon pivot plays, for example, if it does not possess players who are exponents of turn-round and hook shots.

Just as there is no one system of defense that is the complete answer, it is equally true that there is no ideal method of team attack that is suited to every situation. The good basketball team is prepared to modify its attack to meet the particular game situations and defensive tactics of the opponents. At one time in basketball the use of set plays was generally considered to be the be-all and end-all of attack. In this system the players were drilled to such an extent that they could automatically reproduce a certain sequence of movements and passes in order to bring the ball to a predetermined point from which the shot was made. Such a system required that teams had a repertoire of set plays to combat different types of defense. Many amateur teams tried to emulate some of the intricate plays successfully exploited by leading professional teams in the mistaken belief that they were a sure answer to the problems of attack. Unfortunately they failed to realize that the success of any set play, no matter how simple, relied entirely upon the individual skill of the players and not on the innate qualities of the set play itself. In the learning stage of basketball few players had sufficient technical ability to ensure that the set play would not break down before reaching its culmination.

With the exception of the fast-break and jump-ball situations, the set play is no longer a prominent feature of attacking methods in modern basketball. Apart from the fact that alert defenses can readily adapt their defensive methods to counter a set play (especially in big-time basketball where scouting of opponents enables the coach to plan defensive measures in advance), the amount of practice required to perfect a set play is out of proportion to the advantage that can be gained. Furthermore, it has been repeatedly asserted that basketball is a game in which split-second reaction to given opportunities is essential to success. If teams are drilled to conform to a specific pattern regardless of the situation, many opportunities will be forfeited not to mention the confusion that may result if the play fails to work and the team has no alternative method of attack. It is far better for teams to have a general pattern of attack that is built upon good passing, good movement about the court and, above all, good shooting ability.

Court Balance

As a general rule there should be an overall balance of floor space observed in attack, not only in the interests of establishing a sound attack but also to ensure a ready switch to defense should possession be lost. If all five attacking players are simultaneously situated in the area close to the basket their opponents may be able to launch an attack against an undefended basket as soon as possession changes hands. Such a situation is obviously dangerous and must be avoided.

The attacking area can be broadly divided into frontal, central and rear corridors as shown in Diagram 35, and the attacking team will deploy its players in these three areas according to the system of attack being used. When the attack is set up players will tend to circulate in their particular corridor of operation and as one player cuts or drives into another corridor his place will be taken by a teammate so that the general pattern of attack is maintained and overall floor balance preserved.

There are numerous combinations of allocating five attackers to the three corridors and the actual system used at any time must always bear relation to the tactics of the defenders and the talents of the attackers. Each variation has its own strengths and weaknesses and the suitability can only be judged by the actual circumstances at the time. Probably the most fundamental system is the two-two-one attack in which two players form a safety line in the rear corridor, two more circulate in the central area and one player operates across the basket area. This system is flexible enough to be adapted to meet man-to-man, zone or combination defenses and permits an effective switch

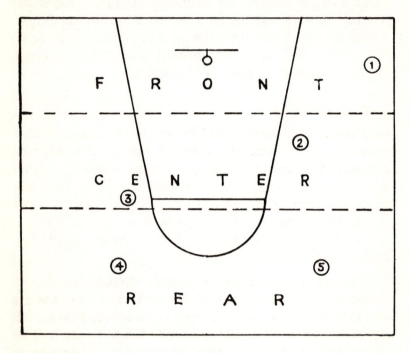

DIAGRAM 35

from attack to defense as soon as possession of the ball is lost. However, in different circumstances, other arrangements of the five attackers may be preferred and this can only be determined by the evidence of the game in progress. At all times the pattern of attack should be suited to make the utmost of its own strength and to exploit fully any weaknesses in the opposing defense.

Attacking Play against Basic Man-to-Man Defense

When opposed by basic man-to-man defense the players in the attacking team are individually guarded by one opponent whose primary objective, in general, is to keep between the attacker and the basket. Given good individual techniques and the ability to create and accept scoring opportunities the most effective tactics against basic man-to-man defense is undoubtedly screen play. By setting up a temporary obstacle to divide the guard from his respective attacker the team has one man momentarily unmarked who can break for the basket or other scoring position. For screen play to be successful it is important that those players not involved in the screen keep the basket area clear of congestion so that the scoring lanes are left open.

Attacking Play against a Zone Defense

In zone defense the defenders concentrate upon the ball and react to its movement rather than the movement of the attackers. The great weakness of any zone defense is that it has no answer to good outside shooting and any team that has players who excel in this department should exploit this fundamental weakness. Assuming the attackers are proficient handlers, the ball can be moved around the zone more quickly than the defenders can adjust their floor positions to cover the new handler. This discrepancy will give the expert shooter ample time to take an uninterrupted shot at the basket. Furthermore, if the zone is forced to spread in an effort to meet the threat of outside shooting the defenders will increase their areas of responsibility and be far more susceptible to penetration.

Another form of attack that pays dividends against a zone defense is one in which the team overloads one part of the zone. By concentrating a number of its players on one side of the zone, the attackers can outnumber the defense because the defenders away from the ball will not move out of their own territory if they are playing on strict zone principles. Through rapid interchange of passes it should then be possible for the numerically superior attackers to get one man free for an uninterrupted shot at the basket. If the defenders do leave their territory to support their outnumbered colleague they will open up shooting lanes for someone else on the other side of the zone.

No matter what tactics are being employed to beat the zone the best results can only be obtained if the attackers are able to move the ball accurately and rapidly. Every zone defense becomes suspect against a team of expert ball handlers.

Fast Break

No matter what style of attack a team may favor as its general pattern it must always be prepared to apply the fast break. If any one system can be accredited the most important method of attack in basketball it must surely be the fast break and every team should be constantly on the lookout for setting one in motion. Indeed, not a few prominent teams regard the fast break as their principal method of attack and only resort to other systems if this breaks down.

The aim of every fast break is for the attackers to get the ball into the close scoring area before the opponents have had time to establish sound defensive positions. If the defense are outnumbered as a result of this strategy it should be possible for one of the attackers to take an uninterrupted shot from close quarters. There are many variations in the interpretation of the fast break and considerable divergence of opinion as to which is the best method. Some coaches advocate the use of quick short passes until the ball arrives in the shooting area; others prefer the ball to be dribbled as soon as it has been passed clear. Both methods have their merits for although the ball travels faster when it is being passed than when it is being dribbled, the latter method enables the players not actually handling the ball to get ahead of the dribbler by the time he has reached the shooting area. No matter what method is used it is of the utmost importance that players know precisely what is expected of them.

The fast break is one set play that should be rehearsed in practice sessions.

A fast-break attack can be initiated more easily if the team itself is using a zone method of defense. In these circumstances each player has an assigned territory on the floor and the player taking the rebound, or bringing the ball in from out-of-bounds,

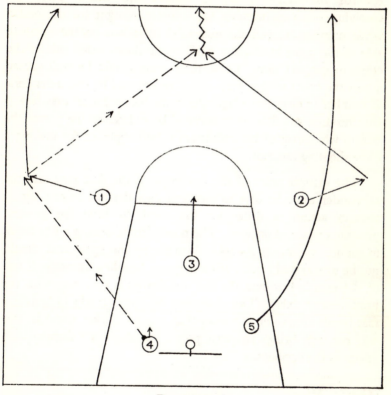

DIAGRAM 36

will know where to find his teammates for the all-important first pass. A typical fast-break attack from a two-one-two zone defence is illustrated in Diagram 36. In this version of a fast break the leading players in the zone, numbers (1) and (2), break towards the side lines in readiness to receive the first pass; this break should be made as soon as it is apparent that the opponents are about to lose possession. On taking the rebound, or bringing the ball in from out-of-bounds, the guard (4) immediately passes it out to the forward player (1) on the nearer side line. The moment he sees which way the first pass is going the other forward player (2) on the opposite side line breaks diagonally towards the center ready to receive the second pass. On receiving this pass number (2) dribbles straight for the basket while number (1) and the guard (5) (who was on the opposite side of the court at the first pass) sweep down either side of the court to support him. These three men should be well spread across the court so that they cannot be covered by two defenders. If number (2) can drive right up to the basket for an easy lay-up shot he does so; if he is challenged by a defender he passes the ball to whichever of his colleagues is better placed for making a close shooting attempt.

The critical point of the fast break is the first pass and the rebounder must be able to take and pass the ball in one simultaneous action in order for the break to have the greatest possible chance of success. The possibility of setting a fast break in motion whenever a basket is made by the opponents should not be overlooked; quite often they can be taken unawares if one of the guards retrieves the ball and brings it into play with the minimum of delay. The alert team is always ready to launch a fast-break attack for it knows that a quick basket taken in this way not only brings two easy points but also has a demoralizing effect on the opponents.

Pivot Play

Pivot play can be featured in most systems of attack and is an invaluable method of setting up scoring opportunities. In its simplest form, the Single Pivot, the play is built around one player who is an expert at the turn-around and hook shots and who can distribute the ball well; it is an added asset if he is a tall man. The pivot player normally positions himself just outside the free-throw lane or on the free-throw line; he has his back to the basket and moves across the area as the play switches from one side to the other. The remaining attackers circulate outside the free-throw lane, passing the ball and screening for each other while watching for the opportunity to throw a pass to the pivot man. When he receives the ball the pivot player can make his shot or immediately pass the ball out to a cutting player or someone who is well placed to make a scoring attempt. A good pivot player is virtually a _must_ for every team in present day basketball; the team that is fortunate enough to have two good pivot players can build up a formidable system of attack.

Attacking Play against Pressing Man-to-Man

When confronted by a pressing man-to-man defense many teams become confused because they do not know how to counter this strategy. As the object of the press is to make it difficult for the attackers to throw and receive passes this is one of the occasions when dribbling is the best answer. If a team possesses a particularly strong dribbler the ball should be passed to him at the outset so that he can use his ability in a straightforward one-on-one situation against his opponent; alternatively, the ball can be passed to an attacker who is being guarded by a weaker player in the opposing team so that this attacker can use the dribble to elude his guard. When opposed by a pressing defense the attackers who are not in possession should keep clear of the basket area, taking their guards with them, so that the ball handler can dribble and drive in to the basket once he has succeeded in getting past his guard. Individual dribbling skill is the keynote to success against a pressing defense; team tactics become an incidental consideration.

Attacking Play at a Jump Ball

Although jump-ball situations no longer assume the same importance as they did in the days when each basket was followed by a center jump, they may be sufficient in number to make the difference between winning and losing in a closely contested game. Teams should have some notion of tactics at every jump ball.

The primary objective at a jump ball is to gain possession of the ball and all members of the team must know where the ball is to be directed should the jumper be successful; any plays that emanate from this are secondary in importance. Two typical

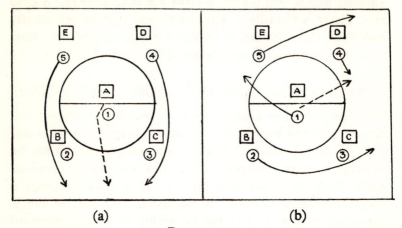

(a)   (b)

DIAGRAM 37

examples of jump-ball plays are illustrated in Diagram 37. As with the fast-break attack, no one set play at a jump ball is necessarily better than another; the important thing is that the team should have some definite tactics and these can be rehearsed during training sessions so that the players know exactly what is expected of them.

In Diagram 37(a), a deep backward play is illustrated in which the jumper endeavors to tap the ball back a considerable distance behind him. Either player 4 or player 5 is assigned to receive the ball and he must cut at the appropriate moment. Players 2 and 3 concentrate on blocking out their respective opponents. As with all similar situations it is essential that the players disguise their intentions and time their movements to take the opponents by surprise.

Another useful jump-ball play is shown in Diagram 37(b) in which the ball is tapped sideways and slightly forward to player 4 who moves to meet the ball. Player 2 cuts behind teammate 3 and player 5 cuts behind opponent D. On receiving the ball player 4 may have the chance of a shot or he may pass the ball to either 2 or 5 depending on the circumstances.

As one set play for all jump ball situations is hardly sufficient to outwit the opposing team for any length of time, the coach may choose to drill his players in a number of different variations. If this is the case it follows that the team must also have a code of signals so that all the players will know which set play is being used each time a jump ball occurs.

ATTACKING DRILLS

Any of the previous drills that culminated in a shooting attempt at the basket can be regarded as an attacking drill; similarly, certain of the defensive drills which involved attacking players can be taken as attacking drills merely by switching the emphasis from one phase to the other. Players can never have too much practice at attacking play and the coach should give as wide a variety of drills as possible so that players develop their attacking ability under all conditions. Each of the following drills caters for a particular aspect of attacking play; many others can be devised.

1. Screening Drill

(Diagram 38)

Five players form up in a semi-circle as shown in Diagram 38 with number 1 holding the ball. He starts the drill by passing the ball to number 2 and then follows up the pass to stand in front of number 2 (blocking the path of his imaginary guard). As soon as number 1 has set the screen number 2 dribbles to the center position, passes to number 3 and then follows up the pass to set a screen for number 3. In the meantime, numbers 1 and 4 exchange places and the drill continues in this way.

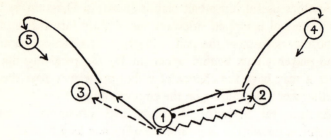

DIAGRAM 38

2. *Cutting and Screening Drill*

(Diagram 39)

Players form up in three files as shown in Diagram 39. Player 1
passes the ball to player A who has cut to a pivot position on the
free-throw lane; number 1 follows up his pass and then cuts
across the free-throw semi-circle to set up a screen for player X.
As soon as the screen has been set player X cuts towards the ball
handler, passing close to the screen, receives a pass and drives in
to the basket for a lay-up shot. Player 1 retrieves the ball, passes
it out to number 2 and the drill continues with the next threesome. Player 1 joins the end of the shooting line, player A joins
the end of the screening line, and player X goes to the end of
the line near the basket.

3. *Tap-In Drill*

(Diagram 40)

Players form up in two files close to the basket as shown in
Diagram 40. Number 1 passes the ball to number 2 who immediately overshoots a lay-up onto the backboard; number 3 leaps
high to tap in the rebound using one or both hands as dictated
by the coach. Player 4 retrieves the ball, passes it to number 5
for him to overshoot a lay-up and the drill continues in this way.
As soon as a player has handled the ball he joins the end of the
opposite line. This is a simple drill but is an ideal way of
practicing tap-ins.

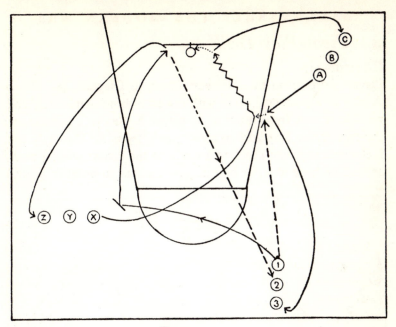

DIAGRAM 39

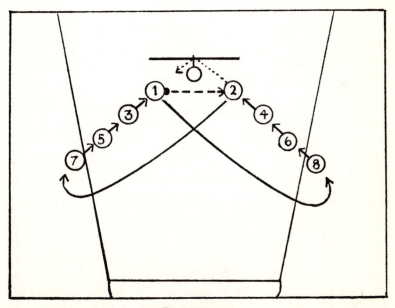

DIAGRAM 40

4. *Pivot-Play Drill*

(Diagram 41)

Players form up in three lines as shown in Diagram 41. Player A cuts to a position in line with the free-throw semi-circle and receives a pass from number 1; player X cuts to a position on the free-throw lane and receives a pass from A. Player X can make an immediate shooting attempt at the basket using a turn-around or hook shot, or he can pass the ball to number 1, who

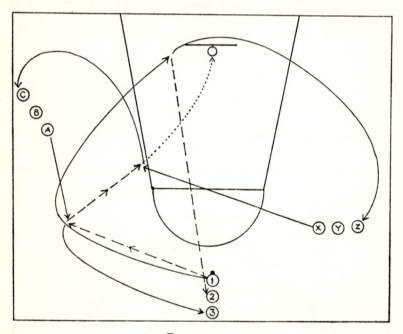

DIAGRAM 41

has cut round A, for him to drive in for a lay-up. Once the players have practiced this drill a number of times the coach should take up a position in the free-throw lane so that he can act as guard on the pivot player and make the drill more realistic. After the shot has been made either player X or player 1 retrieves the ball and passes it out to number 2 so that the drill can be continued by the next threesome; the three players who have just completed the practice join the end of the next file moving in a counterclockwise direction.

5. *Splitting the Post*

This drill is an established favorite with most coaches as it is a fundamental attacking play that can be incorporated into any system of attack. Player 1 takes up a position on the free-throw

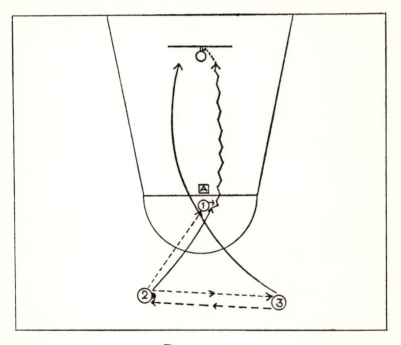

DIAGRAM 42

line with his back to the basket and with a guard standing immediately behind him as shown in Diagram 42; two other players some distance away passing the ball back and forth. Without warning the ball is passed to the post player and the thrower follows up his pass to sweep round the post player; at the same time the third player cuts round the other side of the post player, crossing close behind his colleague. As the two cutters sweep by on either side of him the post player can give a pass to one of them so that a drive and lay-up can be made or he himself can make a shooting attempt at the basket by means of a turn-around or hook shot. This drill calls for good timing on the part of the cutters so that the post player can disguise his intentions from the guard. The post player should also use faking technique to confuse the guard still further.

6 *Training and Coaching Methods*

IT IS a characteristic of the average sportsman that he is content to play games for the sheer enjoyment of them but, for the most part, is opposed to practicing the component skills. Yet, as it is true to say that enjoyment increases as the level of attainment improves, this attitude is illogical. The surest way of developing any physical skill is through intelligent repetition and under no stretch of the imagination can it be justly claimed that playing the game itself affords sufficient repetition of any one aspect, let alone all, to produce a proficient basketball player. The only answer is through repeated practice of the different phases.

The only concession many players are willing to make is a token amount of shooting practice when they first arrive at the court, but even this is discarded as soon as sufficient players are present to get a game under way. Players must be made to realize that practice, more practice and still further practice is necessary if they are to become proficient players. Few players will apply themselves to the rigors of practice and training unless there is outside direction and this is the responsibility of the coach. He is not merely the person who makes the substitutions and gives occasional pep talks during time-out in match play; he is the one who plays the leading part in the development of the players as individuals and the team as a whole. While he may guide the team effort during match play (and a good coach can have considerable bearing upon the outcome of the game), his primary function is to direct training sessions with a view to improving the players' technical ability and building a style of team play.

In the initial stages training will be devoted almost entirely to the acquisition of the various individual skills and it would be difficult to overestimate the value of providing would-be players with the maximum amount of ball-- handling experience. Simplicity should be the keynote of all practices at this stage so that the players and the coach can concentrate on considerations of technique. It is better to spend a little extra time on simple practices so that correct habits are formed from the outset than to try and eradicate faults at a later stage. Once the various fundamentals become automatic their application to game situations and team strategy can be incorporated into the practices. To achieve this, innumerable drills can be devised by the coach along the lines indicated in the previous chapters.

Basketball drills are an invaluable expedient in the acquisition of skill and the gaining of experience. The coach should so present them that his players accept them gladly as an integral part of the learning process and not look upon them as a tiresome routine. Mental attitude toward drills is a significant factor because repetition in itself does not guarantee development of skill; it must be intelligent repetition. In other words, the coach must ensure that his players are aware of the purpose of each drill or practice and execute it with 100 per cent intention of fulfilling the coach's requirements to the best of their ability. A half-hearted, mechanical performance is of no value whatever.

FITNESS FOR BASKETBALL

In every class of basketball physical fitness can augment technical and tactical ability. The higher the standard of play the greater are the physical demands and the top-flight player must be supremely fit if he is to maintain the required level of performance. Match play itself will help to promote fitness but the good coach will incorporate physical conditioning into his training sessions so that the players are better equipped to delay the onset of fatigue. Fatigue causes a rapid deterioration in physical and mental co-ordination and this seriously affects the standard of play.

To a certain extent any training session composed of handling practices, combination drills and a game period will help towards a general conditioning but this is scarcely enough to prepare players for the severe pace of serious competitive play. For this reason it is essential that the coach includes in the training sessions specific activities that are aimed at increasing the stamina, speed and leg strength of the players, because these are the attributes that have the greatest significance for the game. The simplest way of improving the physical condition of the players is for the coach to insist that they do plenty of running during the training session—far more than they will be called upon to do in the course of a game. To this end, many coaches intersperse the different practices with frequent sprints up and down the court, full speed laps of the court dribbling the ball, continuous three-man weaves down the length of the court and similar activities which will increase the vital capacity of the players. If this stamina training is combined with exercises that build up leg power, such as crouch-hops up and down the court or repeated crouch-jumps to touch the backboard or other high point, the coach will ensure that his players are fully prepared to meet the excessive demands of competitive play.

An alternative system preferred by some coaches is one in which the players carry out exclusive conditioning periods outside the normal training sessions so that the latter can be devoted entirely to considerations of play. This system is suitable for those teams in which the players experience no difficulty or hardship in attending a number of sessions during the week (for example, service establishments, colleges, schools, etc.) and it enables the coach to concentrate on building up a high degree of fitness in his players.

The ideal method of conducting these conditioning periods is to use Circuit Training principles. Circuit training, when properly planned and executed, provides a means for deriving the maximum physical benefit in a given period of time. In brief, circuit training is a system of conditioning in which the participants carry out a sequence of set exercises, performing a prescribed number of repetitions of each; the number of repetitions is fixed somewhere below the maximum possible for the individual concerned. Having completed one <u>circuit</u> of the set exercises the person carries out further circuits (usually two more) so that he is truly extended. This system can be made progressive because as fitness improves, and the circuit appears easier, the number of repetitions at each exercise can be stepped up or the time allowed to complete the circuits can be decreased.

To get the maximum benefit from circuit training it is imperative that the exercises are correctly balanced so that recovery from one exercise takes place while the performer is carrying out the next one. Only if this applies can the performer maintain the continuous and sustained effort that is essential in this system. Weights are normally used in circuit training to provide resistance in many of the exercises but non-availability of such equipment does not mean that a coach cannot include this system in his training program. It is possible to devise worthwhile circuits that do not require weights and the following example is one that could well meet the needs of basketball players. The number of repetitions suggested should only be taken as a guide because this factor must always be determined according to the accepted principles of circuit training. For further information on circuit training it is advisable to refer to a detailed explanation of the topic.

Exercises for Basketball Players

1. Stepping—25 repetitions.

From erect positions on the floor players step up to erect positions on a raised surface some 16 to 20 inches above floor level and then return immediately to the floor. The feet are moved in rotation to a rhythmic count of four. (A normal kitchen chair is a suitable height.)

2. Push-ups—10 repetitions.

Players start in the prone support position with the body straight, the feet on the floor and the hands on a raised surface some 6 to 12 inches above floor level. The arms are bent to a right angle and then straightened again.

3. Sprints—5 repetitions.

Players sprint at full speed over a distance of some 12 to 15 yards to touch a given point on the floor with one hand; they immediately sprint back again to touch the floor at the original starting mark. The double journey represents one sprint.

4. Chin-Ups—6 repetitions.

Players grasp a beam, door lintel or other convenient attachment so that the body hangs at full stretch with the feet clear of the floor. The body is pulled upward by the arm muscles until the chin is level with the hands and then lowered again to full stretch.

5. Crouch-Jumps—10 repetitions.

Players start in the crouch position with the fingertips touching the floor. The legs are extended vigorously to jump high in the air with the body fully stretched; the landing is made in the original starting position.

6. Body Bends—20 repetitions.

Players lie down on the floor, on the back, with the body straight and the hands resting on the front of the thighs. The upper part of the trunk is raised, with the head first, until the hands are touching the knees; the trunk is then lowered back down to the starting position.

A series of this nature, if performed two or three times in succession, will provide a strenuous and exacting work-out for a 10 to 15 minute conditioning period.

ORGANIZATION OF THE TRAINING SESSION

To gain the utmost from any training session the coach must plan his program carefully. It is no use going about it haphazardly in the faint hope that sudden inspiration will provide the answer. Players will soon lose interest in training, and respect for the coach, if he persists with the same old routine or can only offer a feeble: "What shall we do now?"

In the first instance the practices and drills will be determined by the existing standard of the team. With beginners, the accent will be on fundamentals; with experienced players it may be on a particular aspect of team play that proved suspect in a previous match. Whatever the level of skill, a common denominator of every training session should be an abundance of purposeful activity. Once the players are assembled and the coach has arrived, the training session should assume a definite pattern with the coach directing operations and the players responding fully to his demands. As a general rule, if the players are past the very elementary stage, the training session should be based on the following outline: —

1. A period of warming-up.
2. Practice of individual skills—general and specialized.
3. Practice of defense and attack fundamentals.
4. Drills in the application of the various skills and fundamentals.
5. Conditioning activities.
6. A period of objective play.
7. A period of uninterrupted play.
8. A period for analysis and discussion.

With the exception of Number 1 the coach may choose to change the order, or omit certain items, depending upon the needs of his players as he sees them at any particular time. However, in principle, these eight headings should represent the coach's guide to basketball training.

1. Warming-Up

In any physical activity it is in the interests of the athlete to prepare his body gradually for forthcoming exertions rather than begin strenuous effort immediately. The player who is not warmed up is sluggish, technically inefficient and far more prone to injury.

Warming-up is often discounted in the basketball training session because players invariably indulge in a certain amount of shooting and other individual skills before the session starts. Indeed, most good coaches give their players specific assignments to practice during this waiting period so that it is objective. Nevertheless, it is a good policy for the coach to give his players a formal period of warming-up, for apart from ensuring that all players are at the right pitch of preparedness, it also helps to set the tone and give an authoritative start to the training session.

As the object of warming-up is literally to warm up the various muscle groups and step up the circulo-respiratory system the activities chosen should be simple, massive and readily interpreted by the players so that involved explanation is not necessary. One method favored by many coaches is the use of simple calisthenics (sometimes called setting-up exercises) as practiced by most athletes and sportsmen before participating in vigorous exercise. Other coaches prefer to give their players a few minutes of uncomplicated ball-handling practices and running drills that are well known to players. When this is the case the activities chosen should be conducted without stoppages or detailed coaching until the coach feels that his players are sufficiently warmed up. The actual method of warming-up is not important and as long as some form of preliminary activity takes place it can be left to the discretion of the individual coach.

2. *Practice of Individual Skills*

The straightforward practice of individual skills is considered by many prominent coaches to be the most important phase of any training session no matter how experienced the players may be. During this part of the session the coach can call upon his players to practice any of the fundamental skills with a view to improving their technique. Opportunity must also be given for the players to specialize so that they can concentrate on eliminating individual weaknesses or developing a particular aspect of their own play that will benefit the team tactics.

3. Practice of Defense and Attack Fundamentals

During this phase of the training session the coach will instruct and drill his players in both the individual and team considerations of defense and attack. The coach must aim at making his players as knowledgeable and competent as possible on all aspects of defense and attack, so that sound teamwork can be built up.

4. Drills

Through the medium of combination drills the coach can improve the technical ability of his players and build a style of team play under game situations. Tactics of defense and attack in all phases of the game can be practiced during this period of the training session.

5. Conditioning

As indicated earlier in this chapter, physical fitness is an important consideration for the basketball player and if there are no specific conditioning sessions it must be provided for during the normal training session along the lines already suggested.

6. Objective Play

Although drills enable the practice of skills and fundamentals to take place under game conditions, the only sure test of their application is in competitive play. In the training session the coach should include a period of basketball play in which two teams play against each other under match conditions but with a particular objective in view. This objective may be concerned with a certain aspect of individual skill, an interpretation of the rules, a specific team tactic of defense or attack or any other consideration as decided by the coach. During this period of objective play the coach will stop the play as and when he chooses in order to check faults, illustrate certain features or generally coach the players.

7. *Uninterrupted Play*

Seldom, if ever, should the coach close a training session without letting the players participate in a period of normal fast basketball play in which there are no interruptions. This is essential not only in preserving the interest and enthusiasm of the players but also in cultivating a correct mental approach to the game. Players must be accustomed to making a sustained effort and not anticipate continual halts. Some coaches may go as far as advocating a period of uninterrupted play, but a short one, in which the whistle is discarded and there are no time-outs whatsoever. They claim that this inculcates a tenacious style of play and enables the players to handle the ball under adverse conditions far in excess of any they will meet in a legally controlled game.

8. *Analysis and Discussion*

A valuable contribution to every training session can be a period of analysis and discussion so that players are encouraged to think positively about the game both at individual and team levels. Quite often doubts and difficulties can be quickly thrashed out this way; without this opportunity a player's progress might well be retarded due to a misunderstanding. It is also true to say that players themselves may frequently proffer suggestions and opinions which will benefit the purpose of the training session. Moreover, active participation in the theoretical approach to the game helps to imbue a team spirit.

CLASS COACHING

One of the criticisms frequently levelled at basketball is the fact that it accommodates only ten players at any given time. While the validity of this criticism cannot be denied it only presents part of the truth. To begin with, in competitive play, very few teams undertake matches with the minimum quota of five players. More often than not a team will have a number of substitutes who will also be brought into the game. Furthermore, it is not unreasonable to claim that even if both teams have the full complement of 12 players it is possible for all 24 of them to derive as much physical exercise in the course of a 40 minute game as is normally achieved by players during a similar period of time in a football game.

In the teaching and coaching of basketball it is possible to utilize a number far in excess of 10 if a little imagination and ingenuity are used. Even on the smallest of courts a typical class of 20 to 30 players can be accommodated as long as sufficient basketballs are available. The various skills and fundamentals of the game can be taught to the class as a whole and then practiced in small groups over the court. The greatest problem may be with regard to shooting technique because, usually, there are only two goals. One answer to this problem is to fix additional goals to the side-walls of the gymnasium to provide additional shooting facilities. For these goals the backboards can be constructed quite easily from a cheap type of rigid board (in the interests of economy and simplicity they can be half the regulation size) and made to fasten on the wall or hook on the wall bars so that they can be removed when not required. There is no need to go to the expense of attaching nets to the rings as these are scarcely justified. With the exception of lay-up shots, goals of this type are quite adequate for practising shooting techniques. Even without these additional goals it is a simple matter to regulate the group activities so that each group in turn practices shooting techniques while the remainder carry out some other phase of the game.

With regard to game play it is possible for four teams of five players each to play simultaneously a modified version of basketball on one court. In this interpretation two opposing teams are restricted to one half of the court; one team assumes the role of attackers while their opponents act as defenders. The attacking team brings the ball in from the half-way mark and normal play proceeds in the one-half of the court until the attackers score a basket or their opponents secure possession of the ball. As soon as this occurs the attackers bring the ball in once again from the half-way mark and the procedure is repeated. After one team has carried out this operation a given number of times the two teams exchange duties. At the same time the other two teams are playing in precisely the same manner in the other half of the court, which means that 20 people altogether are indulging in a form of match play on the one court. It is therefore possible to build up sound techniques and game experience even with a large group of people. It only remains for the coach to provide the opportunity for competitive play and this must be done outside the set class periods.

TESTING AND MEASURING

In addition to competitive play, which is the logical conclusion for the application of the skill acquired in training and practice, the coach can introduce a system of testing and measuring in order to assess the progress and standard of his players. Testing and measuring can be a stimulating adjunct to the training sessions, for apart from providing the coach and players with tangible evidence of technical ability it adds interest, variety and gives the players a real incentive to improve.

No series of practical tests can be 100 per cent accurate in measuring basketball skill because it cannot take into account the many variable factors that arise in competitive play; nor is it possible to devise tests for every phase of the game because many of these cannot be measured objectively. However, a series of standardized tests based on shooting, handling ability and general fitness can help the coach to determine the relative ability of his players and be used to gauge their progress. Once the coach has devised his tests each player should be examined at regular intervals in each of the tests and the results tabulated on a personal record card. These tests must remain constant for a reasonable period of time, ideally throughout the season, so that any deductions made from the statistics are truly informative. On the evidence of the tests, the coach can plan his training sessions so that individual weaknesses can be remedied.

Shooting Tests

Shooting is undoubtedly the most objective of all basketball skills, therefore it is the easiest to test. In order that a reliable evaluation of shooting ability can be made it is recommended that players are tested on at least three different types of shot. One obvious choice is set shooting because it is comparatively easy to regulate, and the following method is one way in which the test can be conducted.

Arcs are marked on the floor at 10, 15 and 20 feet radius from the basket. The players attempt fifteen set shots at each distance, taking five from each of three different floor positions (one central and one to either side) on the arc, so that different angles of approach are tested. When calculating a player's score, allowance should be made for near misses because quite often there is a very fine demarcation between a basket made and a basket missed. Two points for every basket made and half a point if the ball hits the ring but does not enter it is a fair basis of scoring. There is no need to take into account the time factor in this test.

If desired, the coach can adapt this same method to test most of the orthodox shooting techniques. For example, the player can stand on the arc with his back to the basket, receive a pass from the coach and then immediately execute a turn-around or hook shot. Similarly, the player can start from the center circle, dribble the ball to the required position on the arc and attempt a jump shot. When testing any shooting technique in this way, as with the set shot, different ranges and varying angles must be featured so that the player's ability is tested conclusively.

The lay-up shot also lends itself to a form of standardized test. As it is a fundamental skill of the game, requiring all-round handling ability, it is advisable that the coach includes a test that will measure the players' ability in this quarter if his series of tests is to be comprehensive. The test outlined below is one that can be used for this purpose.

The player stands on the side-line opposite the free-throw line and runs in toward the basket; the coach stands on the end-line behind the backboard and passes the ball to the player as he runs in. On receiving the ball the player immediately drives in to the basket, makes a lay-up shot and continues round to a similar starting position on the opposite side-line. He then runs in from this side, receives a pass from the coach (who has already retrieved the ball) and repeats the procedure using the other hand. The test continues in this way for two minutes, the player making as many attempts as he can from each side in turn. For scoring purposes the player receives one point for every basket made; after a brief rest the test is repeated and the points scored in the two efforts will give the player his final mark for the test. With the lay-up shot there should be no question of awarding any points for near misses! By setting a time limit, and permitting the player to make as many lay-ups as he can, this test takes into account both speed and accuracy.

Handling Tests

To a certain degree almost any test of shooting ability must involve a certain amount of general ball-handling technique but the previous tests were concerned primarily with measuring a player's skill at shooting. Numerous tests can be devised that give emphasis to the other considerations of handling and these can be significant in assessing a player's all-round ability at basketball. It is a simple matter to test straightforward dribbling ability and although the following suggested test bears little relation to actual game conditions it can give an accurate indication of the beginner's confidence and ability in dribbling the ball. With experienced players the coach should devise a more searching test to measure skill in this department.

The player stands at one corner of the court and on a starting signal from the coach dribbles diagonally across the court to pass round a player or object that is stationed on the half-way mark of the opposite side line; he continues dribbling, moving diagonally across the court again, until he reaches the corner at the opposite end to his starting position. When he reaches this point he executes a rapid change of direction and continues dribbling down the side line to return to his original starting position where he comes to a legal standstill with the ball. The total time for the journey is noted by the coach and then marks are awarded accordingly. One method of scoring is for the coach to decide upon a performance that merits full marks and then one point can be deducted for each second in excess of this time. The test is then repeated with the player moving in the opposite direction and using his other hand; the two marks gained are added together to give the player his final score for the test.

It is a little more difficult to devise tests that isolate passing and catching ability and one answer is to include composite tests which embrace a wide range of basketball skills in order to account for this phase of the game in the series of tests. Here is one such test that can be used to good purpose in measuring all-round basketball proficiency.

The player starts from one corner of the court on a starting signal from the coach, dribbles in towards the nearer free throw line and performs a legal stop anywhere in the semi-circle. He immediately throws a two-handed pass to the coach, who is standing in the center circle, and then cuts back diagonally across the court towards the half-way mark on the side line, taking a return pass from the coach on the run. On receiving the ball he commences dribbling, passes round a player or object that is stationed on the half-way mark and drives across the court towards the other free-throw line. He comes to a legal standstill anywhere in the semi-circle, executes a pivot and then throws a one-handed pass to the coach. The coach returns the ball immediately and the player takes two free shots from the foul line in quick succession, retrieving the ball himself both times. As soon as he has collected the ball after the second shot he dribbles down the court at full speed; before reaching the free-throw line he must collect the ball on the run and throw a two-handed chest pass at a target behind the end line. This target can be a circle 2 feet in diameter inside another circle 4 feet in diameter, with the common center at approximately chest height, drawn on the end wall, or a board if the wall is too far away.

Controlled speed is an important factor in this test and for scoring purposes the coach must take careful note of the total time consumed from the moment the player starts until the ball hits the target; for each second in excess of a previously determined standard the coach deducts one mark from the maximum. However, as accuracy is also a consideration, bonus marks should be awarded for the basket and target shooting so that players make a genuine effort to succeed. In this respect 5 points should be awarded if both baskets are made and 2 points if only one shot scores; similarly, 5 points are awarded if the ball hits the center circle of the target, but only 2 points if it hits the outer circle. The test is then repeated from the opposite corner so that emphasis switches to the use of the other hand in the dribbling and different angles of approach are used. The two marks are added together to give the player his final score for the test.

A test of this nature can prove a reliable guide to ability as it calls for speed, stamina, passing, shooting and general handling technique, and is one from which players will derive considerable benefit and satisfaction in competing against each other, and themselves, in an effort to achieve a better performance.

Fitness Tests

No system of testing and measuring basketball ability is complete unless it includes fitness tests. A player's physical condition has direct bearing upon his potential in competitive play because his technical efficiency diminishes with the onset of fatigue. As it is in the player's interest to make himself fit for basketball, it is of value for the coach to test this quality.

Perhaps the best way of measuring general fitness is to use the Harvard Stepping Test. In this test the player performs the stepping exercise explained earlier in the chapter and does 150 repetitions in a period of 5 minutes (*i.e.* one every 2 seconds) to a height of 20 inches. On completion of these repetitions the player sits down and the coach takes his pulse count after he has been at rest for one minute; he takes it again after the player has been at rest for two minutes and then finally after four minutes. Each pulse count is taken for a period of half a minute. By adding the three readings together and dividing the result into 15,000 the coach can arrive at a figure which gives a surprisingly accurate comparative index of the player's fitness. As a general guide to the results of this test a normal, healthy person usually arrives at a figure somewhere in the region of 85. The better the physical condition of the person the higher will be the result and supremely fit basketball players can expect to obtain an index of 120 or more. (It is reputed that the incomparable Emil Zatopek, the Czechoslovakian distance runner, once recorded a figure of over 170 when subjected to this test!)

Another useful fitness test that is suitable for basketball players is the Sargent Jump Test because this measures power and jumping ability, both of which are significant factors in the game. One method of applying this test is for the player to hold a piece of chalk in his hand and make a mark on a wall as high as he can reach, while facing it, keeping both feet flat on the floor. He then turns sideways, jumps vertically upwards as high as he possibly can to make another mark on the wall when at the peak of his jump. This is repeated three times and then the coach measures in inches the distance between the original mark and the highest of the other three. The figure obtained can be used to assess the player's score at this test.

Testing and measuring can be of immense value to both the coach and the players but whatever series of tests is devised it cannot be emphasised too strongly that standardization must be a characteristic of each test if the resulting statistics and deductions are to have any degree of reliability. The comparative results of a simple dribbling test, for example, are utterly meaningless if the distance covered by the dribbler is not constant each time the test is carried out. Above all, the coach must remember that testing and measuring is only a means to an end and on no account must it be allowed to dominate the training program. His objective is to improve fundamentals and build a style of play and the only conclusive test and measurement of his success is the evidence of competitive play, not a series of arbitrary tests.

7 Match Play

Function of the Team Coach

If a team is to embark upon every game with the avowed intention of winning—and if this is not the aim then why bother to keep the score?—it cannot afford to enter into competition with a casual or haphazard approach. It is far from axiomatic in basketball that the better team will always win. In the final reckoning the play produced by each team must, of course, depend upon the individual and collective skill of the players but the influence of the team coach can play a major part in deciding the outcome of any game, a factor still not fully appreciated by many of our smaller teams. Time and again one sees players of undoubted ability going on court and being convincingly beaten by lesser opposition simply because their efforts have lacked cohesion and direction. A basketball team without a coach is like an army without a general. The good coach can help his team to make the most of its basketball potential. Many teams in this country combine the duties of the coach with those of captain but this can never be entirely satisfactory. The captain is involved in actual floor play and so is unable to obtain the same overall view of the game as can be achieved by a coach sitting on the bench. In a game such as basketball, which is a continual sequence of changing situations, the guidance of an informed and authoritative observer is indispensable.

As far as match play is concerned, the coach will decide the team tactics to be adopted for each particular game. Every team will develop a general style and quality of play under the guidance of the coach but he should regard each match as an individual encounter and plan the team strategy accordingly. In professional basketball the planning allotted to match play by some of the leading coaches is incredibly thorough and if applied to small teams it could only be regarded as absurd because the existing standard of play does not justify such exhaustive measures. One aspect in particular which illustrates the difference in approach to match play is the relative import- ance attached to scouting of the opposition. To all intents and purposes scouting is disregarded among pros, but it often assumes almost fanatical proportions with coaches en- deavoring to diagnose every aspect of the opponents' play. Not only do they study the team's tactics in every phase of the game but also they prepare a casebook on each individual player in the team. Having acquired this wealth of information the strategy for the forthcoming game is then planned in detail so that the most effective tactics of attack and defense can be put into operation.

We have not yet reached the stage where such analytical methods <u>need</u> be employed—and many people feel that basket- ball ceases to be a game when coaches resort to these extremes —but it is in the best interests of the team if the coach puts a little forethought into the strategy for a forthcoming game. It would be folly, for example, for a coach to ignore the fact that the opponents possess strong outside shooters and let his players commence the game playing a compact zone defense. By the time he has taken steps to adjust the defensive tactics the oppo- nents may have gained a valuable lead which will be sufficient to provide a winning margin. Similarly, if it is known that the opponents favor a zone defense and are rather slow in retreat- ing to their positions the good coach will have alerted his team to the possibility of employing a fast-break attack and will have drilled them in a number of fast-break moves in the pre-match training session. In effect, it is common-sense policy for the coach to ensure that his team has a positive idea of the best mode of attack and defense with which to commence the game and this must always be based upon his knowledge of the particular opponents.

It is the responsibility of the coach, in conjunction with the captain, to select the team to take part in each game, assuming he is fortunate enough to have a choice of players. Ideally, the coach should select a team that is best suited to combat the strengths and exploit the weaknesses of the particular opponents, but in most instances coaches have only a limited number of players at their disposal and it usually resolves itself into picking the players currently in best form to fit into the general pattern of team play. In any case, team selection in basketball is not as final as in other games because the coach is given far more latitude in that he can have up to seven substitutes to call upon. Should it turn out that a selected player is out of form it need not necessarily prove disastrous to the team effort because his place can be taken at any time by one of the substitutes. Over a period of time a coach will get to know his players—far better than they know themselves, in fact—and will be able to judge their form to a fine degree. This judgment will be based upon the standard of play produced in the previous games, in the training sessions preceding the match and on the evidence of their movements as soon as they take the court in the current game.

Before the commencement of any match the coach should prepare his players both physically and mentally for the forthcoming encounter. Any detailed preparation will have been attended to in the pre-match training session but before the players start the game the coach must give them a period of warming-up activities as a safeguard against injuries and inefficient play. Basketball is a game in which top gear must be produced from the word <u>go</u> and any player who goes on the court not adequately warmed up may be unable to keep pace with his teammates, thus causing the team play to break down. When the final warning for the start of the game is given, or at some time before if the players were assembled early and have carried out sufficient warming-up practices, the coach should call them all together and give a final reminder of the team tactics to be adopted in the game. At the same time he should give any special instructions to the players constituting the first line-up regarding their individual duties in attack or defense. As the players will be keyed up the coach should keep this last minute tactical talk brief and to the point. He should not try to cope with all the preparations that should have been accounted for in the pre-match training session. The substitutes can then be instructed to put on their warm top clothing if they have not already done so and the first five players sent on to the court ready to start the game.

Once the game has started the coach is responsible for controlling the time-outs and substitutions of his team and for guiding their play in general. The rules forbid him from giving instructions to the players on the court while play is in progress but skilful use of time-out and substitution will enable the good coach to dictate the pattern of the team play. All too often one sees time-outs and substitutions being taken in a disinterested and automatic fashion, without any real purpose behind them, simply because they are permissible and the coach feels he must use these privileges. Perhaps this is because both these features may seem unsporting to some players and they are unwilling to attach strategical importance to them. Whatever the reason may be, this attitude to time-out and substitution is not justified because not only are they legal but they are also desirable in the interests of preserving the balance of the game. In a game as fast-moving as basketball, the standard of play would suffer if these privileges were abolished.

Normally a coach will let his team play as planned until it becomes obvious that the wrong tactics are being used or individual players are reducing the team potential. In these circumstances a coach may choose to take a time-out in order to make adjustments to the team tactics or make substitutions to improve the line-up. At other times he may call a time-out for a variety of reasons but usually it is to discuss tactical play with the team, offer advice to the players on individual aspects, or make alterations that he thinks will improve the team play. Quite often a time-out can be called to give the players a <u>breather</u>, to upset the rhythm of the opponents or effect an immediate substitution at a critical point in the game. Whenever a time-out is called, including those called by the opponents, the team should converge immediately on the coach to hear what he has to say. Sometimes a comparatively minor suggestion by the coach, such as switching over the defensive responsibilities of two players, can have a far reaching effect on the course of the game. Only the experienced eye of an informed coach sitting on the side-line can perceive such possibilities, hence the part played by the coach assumes great importance.

Half-time can be regarded as an extended time-out in which the coach and players will make a thorough re-assessment of their strategy on the evidence of the first half. Even if the coach does not go to the extent of keeping a shooting chart on both teams so that he knows precisely how and from whereabouts on the floor each basket was scored, he will at least have gained a general impression of these facts. In any case, a glance at the scoresheet will confirm the source of the opponents' baskets and this alone may influence him in making adjustments to the team tactics. A slight change in defensive policy aimed at restricting the opponents' leading goal scorer may be sufficient to swing the balance of the game. Through experience and knowledge of the game the coach will learn to utilize time-outs, and similarly half-time, for the benefit of the team effort.

To a greater or lesser degree, the same principle holds good in the matter of substitution. At certain times when play has stopped the coach may substitute players on and off the court if he so desires. There is no limit to the number of times a player may enter or leave the court in the course of a game (as long as he has not been fouled out of the game) but once again there is little value in utilizing this privilege unless the coach has some objective in view. Indiscriminate substituting may do more harm than good. It is not possible to define an exact code regarding substitution because there are so many conflicting factors to be taken into account. In most cases the aim behind a substitution is to increase the effective play of the team as a whole and the coach may take into account such factors as fatigue, lack of form, special tactics, style of play, and so on, when deciding to substitute one player for another. Sometimes he may even replace a good player by one of lesser ability in order to rest the better player for a later stage in the game or simply to increase the playing experience of his reserve players in the interests of building up a stronger team. So much depends upon the state of the prevailing game that it must always be a question of the coach using his own judgment in relation to the needs of his team.

Without doubt the coach has a difficult and precarious role in match play. If the team loses the game, the blame is invariably attributed to the coach and afterwards he is accused of making bad substitutions and of suggesting the wrong tactics in the time-out discussions. However, when the team wins, it is always due to the good performance on the part of the players and never credited in any way to the coach!

Duties of the Players

In comparison to the coach the duties of the players in match play are straightforward. In the first place they must do their utmost to enter upon every game in top-line condition, and this will be governed by their attitude to training and practice. Secondly, they must always arrive in good time for the start of the game. The player who arrives at the last minute is likely to prove a handicap to the team because he may be unaware of the proposed team strategy, not to mention the fact that he does not leave himself time to get warmed up. Finally, they must give of their best in every phase of their play, accepting without reservation the directions of the coach and captain, and the decisions of the officials. The good player will always submerge personal feelings in the interests of the team.

Duties of the Captain

The captain of a basketball team does not have as prominent a role in match play as pertains to most team games because it is the coach who guides and controls the team strategy. Nevertheless, the captain can exert considerable influence upon the resulting play because it is he who assumes command of the players while on the court. There must be complete understanding between coach and captain so that all tactical decisions of the coach can be implemented in the ensuing floor play. It is essential that the coach and captain work in close harmony in all matters relating to team tactics, selection of players, planning of the training sessions and all other considerations that have bearing on match play so that there is continuity between the theories of the coach and the response of the players. This is the main function of the captain. He is also the team representative on the court of play and he alone can address the officials concerning interpretation of the rules—and only then if it is done in a courteous manner, of course.

Where a team is without a separate coach, the captain must assume the double role and although this is commonplace in a few instances, it is in reality an impossible situation. A captain makes a poor coach because he is unable to view the game as a whole, and a coach makes a poor captain because he cannot concentrate upon his function as a player.

Basketball Rules

As adopted by the National Basketball Committee of the United States and Canada representing the National Collegiate Athletic Association, the National Federation of State High School Athletic Associations, the National Junior College Athletic Association, the Young Men's Christian Association, the Canadian Intercollegiate Athletic Union, and the Canadian Amateur Basketball Association.

Rule 1   Equipment

SECTION 1. The playing court shall be a rectangular surface free from obstructions and with dimensions not greater than 94 feet in length by 50 feet in width.

IDEAL MEASUREMENTS ARE:

High School Age ....50 by 84 feet

College Age ....50 by 94 feet

SECTION 2. The playing court shall be marked with **sidelines, end lines** and other lines as shown on the court diagram (page 4). There shall be at least 3 feet (and preferably 10 feet) of unobstructed space outside.

If, on an unofficial court, there are less than 3 feet of unobstructed space outside any sideline or end line, a narrow broken line shall be marked in the court parallel with and 3 feet inside that boundary. This **restraining line** becomes the boundary line during a throw-in as in 7-6, on that side or end. It continues to be the boundary until the ball crosses the line.

NOTE—It is recommended that both players' benches be placed along that side of the court on which the scorers' table is located. Placing the players' benches outside the end lines should be discouraged.

SECTION 3. The center circle is a circle 2 inches in width and having a radius of 2 feet measured to the inside. A 2-inch wide circle concentric with the center circle shall be drawn with a radius of 6 feet measured to the outside.

SECTION 4. A division line 2 inches wide dividing the court into two parts shall be formed by extending the center circle diameter in both directions until it intersects the sidelines. If the court is less than 74 feet long, it should be divided by two lines, each parallel to and 40 feet from the farther end line.

SECTION 5. A free throw lane, 12 feet wide measured to the outside of each lane boundary and the semicircle with the free throw line as a diameter, shall be marked at each end of the court with dimensions and markings as shown on the court diagram. All bounding lines, but not lane space marks and neutral zone marks, are part of the lane. The color of the lane space marks and neutral zone marks shall contrast with the color of the bounding lines. The lane space marks (2 inches by 8 inches) and neutral zone marks (12 inches by 8 inches) identify areas which extend from the outer edge of the lane lines 36 inches toward the sidelines.

SECTION 6. A free throw line, two inches wide, shall be drawn across each of the circles which have an outside radius of 6 feet as shown on the court diagram. It shall be parallel to the end line and shall have its farther edge 15 feet from the plane of the face of the backboard.

SECTION 7. Each of the two backboards shall be of any rigid material. The front surface shall be flat and, unless it is transparent, it shall be white. The backboard shall be either of two types: (1) A rectangle 6 feet horizontally and 4 feet vertically, or (2) a fan-shaped backboard, 54 inches wide and with dimensions as shown on the diagram.

If the backboard is transparent, it shall be marked as follows: A rectangle shall be centered behind the ring and marked by a 2-inch white line. The rectangle shall have outside dimensions of 24 inches

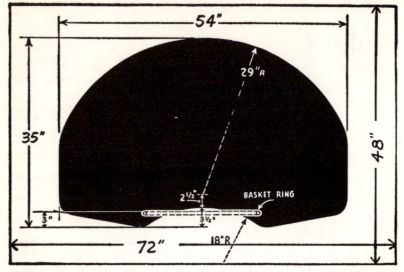

NOTE—Any backboard support, all of which is not directly behind the backboard, should be at least 6 inches behind it if the support extends above the top and at least 2 feet behind it if the support extends beyond the side. Attachment of ring to backboard shall be as prescribed in standards adopted by the Committee and available on request. For the fan-shaped backboard in transparent material, the recurved cut-out at the bottom may be filled in and the ring attached to the front of the backboard.

horizontally and 18 inches vertically. For the rectangular backboard, the top edge of the baseline shall be level with the ring. For the fan-shaped backboard, the baseline shall be omitted and the two vertical lines shall be extended to the bottom of the backboard. (The rectangular target in a bright orange color may be used on a non-transparent backboard.) The border of the backboard shall be marked with a white line. The border shall be 3 inches in width for the rectangular backboard and 3 inches or less in width for the fan-shaped backboard.

For college games, the transparent rectangular backboard shall be used. For other games, either type backboard in either transparent or non-transparent material is legal, but when new equipment is being installed for high school or Y.M.C.A. games, the fan-shaped backboard shall be used.

SECTION 8. Each backboard shall be midway between the sidelines, with the plane of its front face perpendicular to the floor, parallel to the end line and 4 feet from it. The upper edge of the backboard shall be: 13 feet above the floor for the rectangular and 12 feet 8 inches for the fan-shaped backboard.

SECTION 9. The backboards shall be protected from spectators to a distance of at least 3 feet at each end.

SECTION 10. Each basket shall consist of a metal ring, 18 inches in inside diameter, its flange and braces, and a white cord 12-mesh net, 15 to 18 inches in length, suspended from beneath the ring. Each ring shall be not more than ⅝ of an inch in diameter, with the possible addition of small-gauge loops on the under-edge for attaching a 12-mesh net. The ring and its attaching flange and braces shall be bright orange in color. The cord of the net shall be not less than 120-thread nor more than 144-thread seine twine, and shall be so constructed as to check the ball momentarily as it passes through.

SECTION 11. Each basket ring shall be securely attached to the backboard. It shall have its upper edge 10 feet above and parallel to the floor and shall be equidistant from the vertical edges of the backboard. The nearest point of the inside edge of the ring shall be 6 inches from the plane of the face of the backboard.

SECTION 12. The ball shall be spherical. Its color shall be the approved orange shade or natural tan. For college games, it shall have a leather cover unless the teams agree to use a ball with a composition cover. For high school or Y.M.C.A. games, it shall have a leather or composition cover. It shall be of the molded type. If the panels are leather, they shall be cemented to the spherically molded fabric which surrounds an air-tight rubber lining. Its circumference shall be within a maximum of 30 inches and a minimum of 29½ inches for adults and within a maximum of 29½ inches and a minimum of 29 inches for players below senior high school age. Its weight shall be not less than 20 nor more than 22 ounces. It shall be inflated to an air pressure such that when it is dropped to a solid wood floor from a height of six feet, measured to the bottom of the ball, it will rebound to a height, measured to the top of the ball, of not less than 49 inches when it strikes on its least resilient spot nor more than 54 inches when it strikes on its most resilient spot.

NOTE—To be legal, a ball must be tested for resilience at the factory and the air pressure which will give the required reaction must be stamped on it. The pressure for game use must be such as to make the ball bounce legally.

SECTION 13. The home team shall provide a ball which meets the specifications of section 12. If the ball is not legal, the referee may select for use a ball provided by the visiting team.

Rule 2 Officials and Their Duties

SECTION 1. The officials shall be a referee and an umpire, who shall be assisted by two timers and by two scorers. A single timer and a single scorer may be used if they are trained men acceptable to the referee.

NOTE—The officials should wear uniforms distinct from those of either team.

SECTION 2. The referee shall inspect and approve all equipment, including court, baskets, ball, backboards, timers' and scorers' signals. Prior to the scheduled starting time of the game, he shall designate the official timepiece, its operator, the official scorebook and official scorer. He shall be responsible for notifying each captain 3 minutes before each half is to begin.

The referee shall not permit any player to wear equipment which, in his judgment, is dangerous to other players. Elbow, hand, finger, wrist or arm guard, cast or brace made of sole leather, plaster, metal or any other hard substance, even though covered with soft padding, shall always be declared illegal.

Any equipment, which is unnatural and designed to increase a player's height or reach or to gain an advantage, shall not be used.

SECTION 3. The referee shall toss the ball at center to start the game. He shall decide whether a goal shall count if the officials disagree. He shall have power to forfeit a game when conditions warrant. He shall decide matters upon which the timers and the scorers disagree. At the end of each half he shall check and approve the score. His approval at the end of the game terminates the jurisdiction of the officials.

SECTION 4. The referee shall have power to make decisions on any points not specifically covered in the rules.

SECTION 5. The officials shall conduct the game in accordance with the rules. This includes: notifying the captains when play is about to begin at the start of the game, following an intermission or charged time-out, or after any unusual delay in putting the ball in play; putting the ball in play; determining when the ball becomes dead; prohibiting practice during a dead ball, except between halves; administering penalties; ordering time-out; beckoning substitutes to enter the court; warning a team for lack of sufficient action; signaling the point value of a goal by raising one or two fingers to face level and silently counting seconds to administer rules 4-11, 7-6, 8-4, 9-1, 9-7, 9-8, and 10-1-(c).

SECTION 6. The officials shall penalize unsportsmanlike conduct by any player, coach, substitute, team attendant or follower. If there is flagrant misconduct, the officials shall penalize by removing any offending player from the game and banishing any offending coach, substitute, team attendant or follower from the vicinity of the court. A player who commits his fifth personal foul shall also be removed from the game.

SECTION 7. Neither official shall have authority to set aside or question decisions made by the other within the limits of his respective outlined duties.

SECTION 8. The officials shall have power to make decisions for infractions of rules committed either within or outside the boundary lines; also at any moment from 10 minutes before the scheduled starting time of the game to the referee's approval of the final score. This includes the periods when the game may be momentarily stopped for any reason.

SECTION 9. (a) When a foul occurs, an official shall signal the timer to stop his watch and he shall designate the offender to the scorers and indicate with his fingers the number of free throws. The offending player shall raise his hand at arm's length above his head.

(b) When a team is entitled to a throw-in, an official shall clearly signal the act which caused the ball to become dead, the throw-in spot unless it follows a successful goal or an awarded goal, and the player or team entitled to the throw-in. The official shall hand (not toss) the ball to the thrower-in for a throw-in unless the throw-in is from outside an endline following a successful goal.

SECTION 10. Officials may correct an error if a rule is inadvertently set aside and results in: (a) failure to award a merited free throw; or (b) awarding an unmerited free throw; or (c) permitting a wrong player to attempt a free throw; or (d) attempting a free throw at the wrong basket; or (e) erroneously counting or canceling a score. If such error is made while the clock is stopped, it must be recognized before the clock is next started. If the error is made while the clock is running, it must be recognized before the second live ball after the error.

If the error is a free throw by the wrong player, or at the wrong basket or the awarding of an unmerited free throw, the free throw and the activity during it, other than unsportsmanlike conduct, shall be canceled. However, other points scored, consumed time and additional activity, which may occur prior to the recognition of a mistake, shall not be nullified. Errors because of free throw attempts by the wrong player or at the wrong basket shall be corrected by applying rule 8-1 and 2.

If an error, which occurs while the clock is running, is corrected, play shall be resumed from the point at which it was interrupted to rectify the error.

NOTE—Having more than five squad members participating simultaneously, or participating after having been notified that he is disqualified, or a player participating after changing his number, without reporting it to the scorers and an official, are infractions which shall also be penalized if discovered during the time a provision is being violated. (See penalty following Rule 10, Sec. 7.)

SECTION 11. The **scorers** shall record the field goals made, the free throws made and missed, and shall keep a running summary of the points scored. They shall record the personal and technical fouls called on each player and shall notify the referee immediately when the fifth personal foul is called on any player. They shall record the time-outs charged to each team, and shall notify a team and its coach through an official whenever that team takes a fifth charged time-out. They shall signal the nearer official each time a team is granted a charged time-out in excess of the legal number and when a player commits a common foul after his team has been charged with its 4th or 6th personal foul during the half. The scorebook of the home team shall be the official book, unless the referee rules otherwise. The scorers shall compare their records after each goal, each foul and each charged time-out, notifying the referee at once of any discrepancy. If the error cannot be found, the referee shall accept the record of the official book, unless he has knowledge which permits him to decide otherwise. If the discrepancy is in the score and the error is not resolved, the referee shall accept the progressive team totals of the official scorebook.

The scorers shall keep a record of the names and number of players who are to start the game and of all substitutes who enter the game. When there is an infraction of the rules pertaining to submission of the roster, substitutions or numbers of players, they shall notify the nearer official.

The scorers shall use a horn or other device unlike that used by the officials or timers to signal the officials. This may be used immediately if (or as soon as) the ball is dead, or is in control of the offending team.

NOTE—The **Rules Committee** strongly recommends that the official scorer wear a **black and white striped garment** and that his location be clearly marked.

SECTION 12. The **timers** shall note when each half is to start and shall notify the referee more than three minutes before this time so that he may notify the teams, or cause them to be notified, at least three minutes before the half is to start. They shall signal the scorers three minutes before starting time. They shall record playing time and time of stoppages as provided in the rules.

The timers shall be provided with at least one stopwatch which shall be the game watch and which shall be operated by one of the timers, but so placed that both may see it.

The game watch shall be started as prescribed in rule 5-10.

Fifteen seconds before the expiration of an intermission, a charged time-out or a time-out for replacing a disqualified player, the timer shall sound a warning signal immediately after which the players shall be ready to resume play.

The game watch shall be stopped: at the expiration of time for each period, and when an official signals time-out as in 5-8. For a charged time-out, timers shall start a time-out watch and shall direct the scorers to signal the referee when it is time to resume play.

Expiration of playing time in each quarter, half or extra period shall be indicated by the timer's signal. This signal terminates player activity. If the timer's signal fails to sound, or is not heard, the timers shall go on the court or use other means to notify the referee immediately. If, in the meantime, a goal has been made or a foul has occurred, the referee shall consult the timers. If the timers agree that time expired before the ball was in flight, the goal shall not count. If they agree that the period ended (as in 5-6 (b)) before the foul occurred, the foul shall be disregarded unless it was unsportsmanlike. If the timers disagree, the goal shall count or the foul shall be penalized unless the referee has knowledge which alters such ruling.

NOTE—The use of an electric timing device is hereby authorized, together with such modifications in the foregoing as are essential to its operation. If two watches are used, one timer should operate the game watch and signal, and the other should serve as checker of the game watch and operator of the time-out watch.

Ques.—Should timers tell players or coaches how much time remains? Ans.—On request of a captain, an official should give this information to both teams when the ball is dead and time is out.

Rule 3   Players and Substitutes

SECTION 1. Each team consists of 5 players, one of whom is the captain.

Ques.—May a team play with less than 5 players? Ans.—A team must begin with 5 players, but if it has no substitutes to replace disqualified players, it must continue with less than 5.

SECTION 2. The captain is the representative of his team and may address an official on matters of interpretation or to obtain essential information, if it is done in a courteous manner. Any player may address an official to request a time-out (5-8-Item 3) or permission to leave the court.

At least 10 minutes before scheduled starting time each team shall supply the scorers with name and number of each squad member who may participate.

At least 3 minutes before scheduled starting time each team shall designate its 5 starting players.

Failure to comply with either one of these provisions is a technical foul (team), unless the referee considers the failure unavoidable.

SECTION 3. A substitute who desires to enter shall report to the scorers, giving his name and number. If entry is at any time other than between halves, and a substitute, who is entitled and ready to enter, reports to the scorers before change of status of the ball is about to occur, the scorers shall sound the horn if (or as soon as) the ball is dead and time is out. The substitute shall remain outside the boundary until an official beckons him, whereupon he shall enter immediately. If the ball is about to become alive, the beckoning signal should be withheld. The entering player shall not replace a free thrower or a jumper except as stated in 6-3-c, d and e and 8-2 and 3. If he enters to replace a player who must jump or attempt a free throw, he shall withdraw until the next opportunity to substitute.

A player who has been withdrawn may not reenter before the next opportunity to substitute after the clock has started following his replacement.

Ques. (1)—When does a substitute become a player? Ans.—When he legally enters the court.

Ques. (2)—Following substitutions, should the official line up players to aid them in locating opponents? Ans.—This should be avoided if possible but may be done at the request of a captain when three or more substitutes for the same team enter during an opportunity to substitute.

SECTION 4. Each player shall be numbered on the front and back of his shirt with plain numbers of solid color contrasting with the color of his shirt, and made of material not less than ¾ inch wide. The number on the back shall be at least 6 inches high and that on the front at least 4 inches high. Neither of the single digit numbers (1) or (2) nor any digit greater than 5 shall be used, nor shall players on the same team wear identical numbers.

Ques. (1)—If contesting teams have suits of the same color, what shall be done? Ans.—If possible, each team should have two sets of suits, one of light color and the other dark. The light color is for home games. The team which violates this policy should change. If there is doubt, the officials should request the home team to change; on a neutral floor the officials decide.

Ques. (2)—What is the penalty for wearing an illegal number? Ans.—The penalty is a technical foul if the player enters the game, and the infraction is discovered before the clock starts, and if no penalty has been enforced against the player's team in that game for a like violation.

Ques. (3)—May the numbers on the shirt have a border? Ans.—Yes. However, the committee strongly recommends the border be no wider than ¼ inch.

Rule 4   Definitions

SECTION 1. A basket is the 18-inch ring, its flange and braces and appended net through which players attempt to throw the ball. A team's own basket is the one into which its players try to throw the ball. The visiting team shall have the irrevocable choice of baskets at which it may practice before the game and this basket shall be its choice for the 1st half. The teams shall change baskets for the 2nd half.

SECTION 2. Blocking is personal contact which impedes the progress of an opponent who does not have the ball.

SECTION 3. Change of status is the time at which a dead ball becomes alive or a live ball becomes dead. Change of status is about to occur when:

a. A player has started to make a throw-in; or
b. 80% of the time limit count has expired; or
c. An official is ready to make the toss for a jump; or
d. An official starts to place the ball at the disposal of a free thrower.

SECTION 4. A player is in control when he is holding a live ball or dribbling it.

A team is in control when a player of the team is in control and also while a live ball is being passed between teammates. Team control continues until: the ball is in flight after a try for goal; or an opponent secures control; or the ball becomes dead. There is no team control: during a jump ball; a throw-in; during the tapping of a rebound; or after the ball is in flight following a try for goal. In these situations, team control is reestablished when a player secures control.

SECTION 5. A disqualified player is one who is barred from further participation in the game because of committing his fifth personal foul, or a flagrant foul, or for infraction of Rule 10-4 (a) or (b).

SECTION 6. A dribble is ball movement caused by a player in control who throws, bats or taps the ball in the air and/or throws, bats or pushes the ball to the floor and then catches it or touches it once or several times before catching it. The dribble ends when the dribbler: (a) catches the ball in one or both hands; or (b) touches the ball with both hands simultaneously; or (c) loses control as indicated in rules 4-4 and 9-5.

An air dribble is that part of a dribble during which the dribbler throws or taps the ball in the air and then touches it before it touches the floor or is caught.

Ques. (1)—Is a player dribbling while tapping the ball during a jump, or when a pass rebounds from his hand, or when he fumbles, or when he taps a rebound or a pass away from other players who are attempting to get it? Ans.—No. The player is not in control under these conditions.

Ques. (2)—Is it a dribble when a player stands still and: (a) bounces the ball; or (b) holds the ball and touches it to the floor once or more? Ans.—(a) Yes. (b) No.

Ques. (3)—May a dribbler alternate hands? Ans.—Yes.

SECTION 7. **Extra period** is the extension of playing time necessary to break a tie score.

SECTION 8. **a.** **A foul** is an infraction of the rules, the penalty for which is one or more free throws unless it is a double foul, or is a player control foul, in which case the free throw provision is cancelled. For convenience, a personal foul, which is neither flagrant nor intentional nor committed against a player trying for field goal, nor a part of a double or multiple foul, is termed a **common foul.**

b. **A double foul** is a situation in which two opponents commit personal fouls against each other at approximately the same time. A **false double foul** is a situation in which there are fouls by both teams, the second of which occurs before the clock is started following the first, but such that at least one of the attributes of a double foul is absent.

c. **A flagrant foul** is an unsportsmanlike act and may be a personal or technical foul of a violent or savage nature, or a technical non-contact foul, which displays vulgar or abusive conduct. It may or may not be intentional.

d. **An intentional foul** is a personal foul, which in the judgment of the official appears to be designed or premeditated. It is not based on the severity of the act.

e. **A multiple foul** is a situation in which two or more teammates commit personal fouls against the same opponent at approximately the same time. A **false multiple foul** is a situation in which there are two or more fouls by the same team and such that the last foul is committed before the clock is started following the first, and such that at least one of the attributes of a multiple foul is absent.

f. **A personal foul** (10-8) is a player foul which involves contact with an opponent while the ball is alive or after the ball is in possession of a player for a throw-in.

g. **A player control foul** is a common foul committed by a player while he or a teammate is in control.

h. **A technical foul** (10-1 to 7) is: a foul by a non-player, or a player foul which does not involve contact with an opponent, or a player foul which involves unsportsmanlike contact with an opponent while the ball is dead, except as indicated in last clause of (d) above.

i. **An unsportsmanlike foul** is a technical foul which consists of unfair, unethical or dishonorable conduct.

SECTION 9. **A free throw** is the privilege given a player to score one point by an unhindered try for goal from within the free throw circle and behind the free throw line. A free throw starts when the ball is given to the free thrower at the free throw line or is placed on the line. It ends when: the try is successful; or it is certain the try will not be successful; or when the try touches the floor or any player; or when the ball becomes dead.

SECTION 10. (a) **A team's front court** consists of that part of the court between its end line and the nearer edge of the division line and including its basket and the inbounds part of its backboard. **A team's back court** consists of the rest of the court including its opponents' basket and inbounds part of the backboard and the entire division line.

(b) **A live ball is in the front or back court** of the team in control as follows: (1) A ball which is in contact with a player or with the court is in the back court if either the ball or the player (either player if the ball is touching more than one) is touching the back court. It is in the front court if neither the ball nor the player is touching the back court. (2) **A ball which is not in contact** with a player or the court retains the same status as when it was last in contact with a player or the court.

> Ques.—From the front court, A passes the ball across the division line. It touches a teammate who is in the air after leaping from the back court or it touches an official in the back court? Is the ball in the back court? **Ans.—** Yes. See 4-15.

SECTION 11. **Held ball** occurs when:

a. Opponents have hands so firmly on the ball that control cannot be obtained without undue roughness; or

b. A closely guarded player anywhere in his front court holds the ball for 5 seconds; or

c. A team, in its front court, controls the ball for 5 seconds in an area enclosed by screening teammates; or

d. In an attempt to consume time, a closely guarded player within a few feet of a front court boundary intersection dribbles, or combines dribbling and holding the ball for 5 seconds; or

e. In an attempt to consume time, a closely guarded player, in his mid-court area, dribbles, or combines dribbling and holding the ball for 5 seconds.

The player in control is closely guarded when his opponent is in a guarding stance at a distance not exceeding 6 feet from him.

> Ques.—Is it a held ball merely because the player holding the ball is lying or sitting on the floor? Ans.—No.

SECTION 12. **Holding** is personal contact with an opponent which interferes with his freedom of movement.

SECTION 13. **A jump ball** is a method of putting the ball into play by tossing it up between two opponents in one of the three circles. It begins when the ball leaves the official's hand, and ends as outlined in rule 6-4.

SECTION 14. **Lack of sufficient action** is the failure of the responsible team to force play.

SECTION 15. **The location of a player** (or non-player) is determined by where he is touching the floor as far as being inbounds or out of bounds or being in the front court or back court is concerned. When he is in the air from a leap, his status with reference to these two factors is the same as at the time he was last in contact with the floor or an extension of the floor such as a bleacher. When the ball touches an official, it is the same as touching the floor at the official's location.

SECTION 16. **The mid-court** area of a team is that part of its front court between the division line and a parallel imaginary line approximately 3 feet outside that part of the free throw circle which is farthest from the end line.

SECTION 17. **A multiple throw** is a succession of free throws attempted by the same team.

SECTION 18. **A pass** is movement of the ball caused by a player, who throws, bats or rolls the ball to another player.

SECTION 19. **A penalty** for a foul is the charging of the offender with the foul and awarding one or more free throws, or awarding the ball to the opponents for a throw-in. The penalty for a violation is the awarding of the ball to the opponents for a throw-in or one or more points or a substitute free throw.

SECTION 20. **A pivot** takes place when a player who is holding the ball steps once or more than once in any direction with the same foot, the other foot, called the pivot foot, being kept at its point of contact with the floor.

SECTION 21. **A rule** is one of the groups of laws which govern the game. A game law (commonly called a rule) sometimes states or implies the ball is dead or a foul or violation is involved. If it does not, it is assumed the ball is alive and no foul or violation has occurred to affect the given situation. A single infraction is not complicated by a second infraction unless so stated or implied.

SECTION 22. Running with the ball (traveling) is moving a foot or the feet in any direction in excess of prescribed limits while holding the ball. The limits follow:

Item 1. A player who receives the ball while standing still may pivot, using either foot as the pivot foot.

Item 2. A player, who receives the ball while his feet are moving or who is dribbling, may stop as follows:
(a) If he catches the ball while both feet are off the floor and:
 (1) **He alights with both feet** touching the floor simultaneously, he may pivot using either foot as the pivot foot; or
 (2) **He alights with first one foot** touching the floor followed by the other, he may pivot using the first foot to touch the floor as the pivot foot; or
 (3) **He alights on one foot,** he may jump off that foot and alight with both feet simultaneously but he may not pivot before releasing the ball.
(b) If he catches the ball while only **one foot** is off the floor:
 (1) **He may step** with the foot which is off the floor and may then pivot using the other foot as the pivot foot; or
 (2) **He may jump** with the foot which is on the floor and alight with both feet simultaneously, but he may not pivot before releasing the ball.

Item 3. After a player has come to a stop, he may pass or throw for goal under the following conditions:
(a) In Items 1, 2a(1), 2a(2) and 2b(1), he may **lift either foot,** but if he lifts his pivot foot or jumps before he passes or throws for goal, the ball must leave his hand before the pivot foot again touches the floor; or if he has jumped before either foot touches the floor.
(b) In Items 2a(3) and 2b(2), he may **lift either foot or jump** before he passes or throws for goal. However, the ball must leave his hand before a foot which has left the floor retouches it.

Item 4. A player who receives the ball as in Item 1 or a player, who comes to a stop after he receives the ball while he is moving his feet, may start a dribble under the following conditions:
(a) In Items 1, 2a(1), 2a(2) and 2b(1), the ball must leave his hand **before the pivot foot leaves the floor.**
(b) In Items 2a(3) and 2b(2), the ball must leave his hand **before either foot leaves the floor.**

Ques. (1)—Is it traveling, if a player falls to the floor while holding the ball? Ans.—No, unless he makes progress by sliding.
Ques. (2)—A1 jumps to throw the ball. B1 prevents the throw by placing one or both hands firmly on the ball so that: (a) A1; or (b) A1 and B1 both return to the floor holding it. Ans.—Held ball. However, if A1 voluntarily drops the ball before he returns to the floor and he then touches the ball before it is touched by another player, A1 has committed a traveling violation.

SECTION 23. A screen is legal action by a player who, without causing contact, delays or prevents an opponent from reaching a desired position.

SECTION 24. A throw-in is a method of putting the ball in play from out of bounds in accordance with Rule 7. The throw-in begins when the ball is at the disposal of the player or team entitled to it and ends when the passed ball touches or is touched by an inbounds player other than the thrower-in.

Section 25. A try for field goal is an attempt by a player to score 2 points by throwing the ball into his basket. The try starts when the player begins the motion which habitually preceeds the release of the ball. The try ends when the ball is clearly in flight.

SECTION 26. A violation is a rule infraction of the type listed in Rule 9.

Rule 5 Scoring and Timing Regulations

SECTION 1. **A goal** is made when a live ball enters the basket from above and remains in or passes through.

Ques.—If the ball enters the basket from below, goes through and drops back into the basket, is a goal scored? Ans.—No, it is a violation.

SECTION 2. **A goal from the field** counts 2 points for the team into whose basket the ball is thrown. A goal from a free throw is credited to the thrower and counts 1 point for his team.

NOTE—A field goal in A's basket after being last touched by B is not credited to any player but is mentioned in a footnote and two points are added to A's total.

Ques.—A player throws a field goal in his opponents' basket. Who gets credit for the goal? Ans.—It is not credited to a player. It is added to the opponents' score and mentioned in a footnote.

SECTION 3. **The winning team** is the one which has accumulated the greater number of points when the game ends.

SECTION 4. **The referee shall forfeit** the game if a team refuses to play after being instructed to do so by either official. If the team to which the game is forfeited is ahead, the score at the time of forfeiture shall stand. If this team is not ahead the score shall be recorded as 2-0 in its favor.

Ques.—When the game is forfeited, are the points made by each player credited to him? Ans.—The league officers should decide. It is customary to include such points in the scoring records.

SECTION 5. **Playing time** shall be: (a) for teams of college age, two halves of 20 minutes each with an intermission of 15 minutes between halves; (b) for teams of high school age, four quarters of 8 minutes each with intermissions of one minute after the 1st and 3rd quarters and 10 minutes between halves; (c) for teams younger than in (b), four quarters of 6 minutes each with intermissions the same as for (b).

SECTION 6. **Each period** begins when the ball first becomes alive. It ends when time expires except that: (a) if the ball is in flight after a try for field goal, the period ends when the ball goes through the basket; or it is certain the ball will not go through the basket; or when the ball, after the try is in flight, touches the floor or any player; or when the ball becomes dead; or (b) if a held ball occurs so near the expiration of time that the clock is not stopped before time expires, the period ends with the held ball; or (c) if a foul occurs so near the expiration of time that the timer cannot get the clock stopped before time expires or if the foul occurs after time expires but while the ball is in flight on a try for field goal, the period ends when the free throw or throws and all related activity have been completed.

SECTION 7. **If the score is tied** at the end of the second half, play shall continue without change of baskets for one or more extra periods with a one-minute intermission before each extra period. The game ends if, at the end of any extra period, the score is not tied.

In games played in halves, the length of each extra period shall be 5 minutes. **In games played in quarters,** the length of each extra period shall be 3 minutes. As many such periods as are necessary to break the tie shall be played. Extra periods are an extension of the 2nd half.

Ques.—With the score tied, a foul is committed near the expiration of time in the second half. If the free throw is successful, should an extra period be played? Ans.—If the foul occurs before the ball becomes dead and the period is ended as outlined in 5-6, no extra period is played. But if the foul occurs after the period has clearly ended, the extra period is played.

SECTION 8. **Time-out** occurs and the game watch, if running, shall be stopped when an official:

Item 1. Signals: (a) a foul; (b) held ball; or (c) a violation.

Item 2. Stops play: (a) because of an injury; (b) to confer with scorers or timers; (c) because of unusual delay in getting a dead ball alive; or (d) for any emergency.

Item 3. Grants a player's request for a time-out, such request being granted only when the ball is dead or in control of a player of his team and when no change of status of the ball is about to occur.

Item 4. Responds to the scorer's signal to grant a coach's request that a correctable error be prevented or rectified. Such a request shall be presented while the ball is dead and the clock is stopped. The appeal to the official shall be presented at the scorer's table when a coach of each team may be present.

NOTE—When a player is injured as in Item 2(a), the official may suspend play when the ball is dead or is in control of the injured player's team or when the opponents complete a play. A play is completed when a team loses control (including throwing for goal), or withholds the ball from play by ceasing to attempt to score or advance the ball to a scoring position. When necessary to protect an injured player, the official may suspend play immediately.

SECTION 9. A time-out shall be charged to a team for each minute or fraction of a minute consumed under Items 2(a), 3 and 4 of Section 8.

EXCEPTIONS: No time-out is charged:

(a) If in Item 2(a) an injured player is ready to play immediately or is replaced within 1½ minutes; or

(b) If in Item 3 the player's request results from displaced eyeglasses or lens; or

(c) If in Item 4 a correctable error is prevented or rectified; or

(d) If a disqualified player is replaced within 1 minute.

SECTION 10. After time has been out, the game watch shall be started when the official signals time-in. If official neglects to signal, the timer is authorized to start the watch unless an official specifically signals continued time-out.

a. If play is resumed by a jump, the watch shall be started when the tossed ball is legally tapped.

b. If a free throw is not successful and ball is to remain alive, the watch shall be started when the ball is touched or touches a player on the court.

c. If play is resumed by a throw-in, the watch shall be started when the ball touches or is touched by a player on the court.

Ques.—During a free throw which is not successful, a violation occurs. Should the clock be started when the ball is touched or touches a player on the court? Ans.—No and official should avoid using the time-in chopping motion, if the ball is not to remain alive.

SECTION 11. Five charged time-outs may be granted each team during an untied game. During each extra period, each team is always entitled to at least one time-out. Unused time-outs accumulate and may be used at any time. Time-outs in excess of the allotted number may be granted at the expense of a technical foul for each.

Rule 6   Live Ball and Dead Ball

SECTION 1. The game shall be started by a jump ball in the center circle. After any subsequent dead ball, play shall be resumed by a jump ball or by a throw-in or by placing it at the disposal of a free thrower. The ball becomes alive when: (a) on a jump ball, the ball leaves the official's hand; or (b) on a throw-in, the ball touches a player who is inbounds; or (c) on a free throw, the ball is placed at the disposal of the free thrower.

SECTION 2. The ball shall be put in play in the center circle by a jump between two opponents: (a) at the beginning of each quarter and extra period; or (b) after a double foul; or (c) after the last free throw following a false double foul.

Ques.—Does a quarter, half or extra period start with a jump ball if a foul occurs before the ball becomes alive? **Ans.**—No. Any rules statement is made on the assumption that no infraction is involved unless mentioned or implied. If such infraction occurs, the rule governing it is followed in accordance with Rule 4-21.

SECTION 3. The ball shall be put in play by a jump ball at the center of the restraining circle which is nearest the spot where: (a) a held ball occurs; or (b) the ball goes out of bounds as in 7-3; or (c) a double free throw violation occurs; or (d) the ball lodges on a basket support; or (e) the ball becomes dead when neither team is in control and no goal or infraction or end of a period is involved. In (a) or (b), the jump shall be between the two involved players unless injury or disqualification requires substitution for a jumper, in which case his substitute shall jump. In (c), (d), and (e), the jump shall be between any two opponents.

SECTION 4. For any jump ball, each jumper shall have one or both feet on or inside that half of the jumping circle (imaginary if in a free throw restraining circle) which is farther from his own basket. An official shall then toss the ball upward between the jumpers in a plane at right angles to the sidelines, to a height greater than either of them can jump and so that it will drop between them. The ball must be tapped by one or both of the jumpers after it reaches its highest point. If it touches the floor without being tapped by at least one of the jumpers, the official shall toss the ball again.

Neither jumper shall: tap the tossed ball before it reaches its highest point; nor leave the jumping circle until the ball has been tapped; nor catch the jump ball; nor touch it more than twice. The jump ball and these restrictions end when the tapped ball touches one of the eight non-jumpers, the floor, the basket or the backboard.

None of the 8 non-jumpers shall have either foot in the restraining circle cylinder until the ball has been tapped. Teammates may not occupy adjacent positions around the restraining circle if an opponent indicates his desire for one of these positions before the official is ready to toss the ball.

Ques.—During jump ball, is a jumper required to: (a) face his own basket; and (b) jump and attempt to tap the tossed ball? **Ans.**—(a) No specific facing is required. However, a jumper must be in the proper half of the jumping circle. (b) No. But if neither jumper taps the ball, it should be tossed again with both jumpers being ordered to jump.

SECTION 5. The ball shall be put in play by a throw-in under circumstances as outlined in Rules 7, 8-5 and 9-1 to 11.

SECTION 6. The ball shall be put in play by placing it at the disposal of a free thrower before each free throw.

SECTION 7. The ball becomes dead or remains dead when:

a. **Any goal** is made as in 5-1;
b. **It is apparent** the free throw will not be successful: on a free throw for a technical foul or a false double foul, or a free throw which is to be followed by another throw;
c. **Held ball** occurs or ball lodges on the basket support;
d. **Official's whistle** is blown;
e. **Time expires** for a quarter, half or extra period;
f. **A foul occurs;** or
g. **Any floor violation** (9-2 to 10) occurs, or there is basket interference (9-11), or there is a free throw violation by the thrower's team (9-1).

EXCEPTION: The ball does not become dead when: (1) d, e or f occurs after a try for a field goal is in flight; or (2) d or f occurs after a try for a free throw is in flight; or (3) a foul is committed by an opponent of a player who has started a try for goal before the foul occurred provided time did not expire before the ball was in flight. The trying motion must be continuous and begins after the ball comes to rest in the player's hand or hands and is completed when the ball is clearly in flight. The trying motion may include arm, foot, or body movements used by the player when throwing the ball at his basket.

Ques.—If the ball is in flight after A's try for field goal when time for the period expires, and if the ball is subsequently touched, does the goal count if made? **Ans.**—No. The try ends when ball is touched. If it is basket interference (9-11) by B, 2 points are awarded to A.

Rule 7   Out of Bounds and the Throw-In

SECTION 1. A player is out of bounds when he touches the floor or any object on or outside a boundary. For location of a player in the air, see 4-15.

The ball is out of bounds when it touches: a player who is out of bounds; or any other person, the floor, or any object on or outside a boundary; or the supports or back of the backboard; or ceiling, overhead equipment or supports.

NOTE—When the rectangular backboard is used, the ball is out of bounds if it passes over the backboard.

Ques. (1)—Ball rebounds from the edge of backboard and across boundary line, but before it touches the floor or any obstruction out of bounds, it is caught by a player who is inbounds. Is the ball inbounds or out of bounds? **Ans.**—Inbounds.

Ques. (2)—The ball touches or rolls along the edge of the backboard without touching the supports. Is the ball dead? **Ans.**—No, unless ground rules to the contrary have been mutually agreed upon before the game.

SECTION 2. The ball is caused to go out of bounds by the last player to touch it before it goes out, provided it is out of bounds because of touching something other than a player.

If the ball is out of bounds because of touching a player who is on or outside a boundary, such player causes it to go out.

Ques. (1)—Live ball is held by A. (a) The ball held by or passed by A touches B when B is on or outside the boundary; or (b) the ball is batted to out of bounds by B who is inbounds. **Ans.**—Ball awarded to A for a throw-in.

Ques. (2)—Ball passed by A touches an official and goes out of bounds. Whose ball? **Ans.**—B's ball.

SECTION 3. If the ball goes out of bounds and was last touched simultaneously by two opponents, both of whom are inbounds or out of bounds, or if the official is in doubt as to who last touched the ball, or if the officials disagree, play shall be resumed by a jump ball between the two involved players in the nearest restraining circle.

SECTION 4. The ball is awarded out of bounds after: (a) a violation as in Rule 9; or (b) a free throw for a technical foul as in Rule 8-5-b; or (c) a field goal or a successful free throw for personal foul as in 8-5-a or an awarded goal as in 9-11; or (d) the ball becomes dead while a team is in control provided no infraction or the end of a period is involved; or (e) a player control foul.

SECTION 5. a. When the ball is out of bounds after any violation as outlined in sections 2 through 11 in Rule 9, the official shall designate a nearby opponent of the player who committed the violation, and he shall hand the ball to this player or his substitute for a throw-in from the designated spot nearest the violation, except as indicated in the penalties which follow Rule 9-10 and 11.

b. After a dead ball, as listed in section 4 (d), any player of the team in control shall make the throw-in from the designated out of bounds spot nearest to the ball when it became dead.

c. After a player control foul, any player of the offended team shall make the throw-in from the designated spot nearest the foul, except that, if the ball has passed through the basket during the dead ball period immediately following the foul, no point can be scored and the ball is awarded to any player of the offended team out of bounds at either end of that free throw line extended which is nearer the goal through which the ball was thrown.

d. **If in items a, b or c, the throw-in spot is behind a backboard, the** throw-in shall be made from the nearer free throw lane line extended.

e. **After a goal as listed in section 4 (c),** the team not credited with the score shall make the throw-in from the end of the court where the goal was made and from any point outside the end line. Any player of the team may make a direct throw-in or he may pass the ball along the end line to a teammate behind the line.

f. **After a technical foul,** any player of the team to whom the free throw has been awarded shall make the throw-in from out of bounds at mid-court on either side.

g. **After a free throw violation by the throwing team as listed in section 1 of rule 9,** any opponent of the throwing team shall make the throw-in from out of bounds at either end of the free throw line extended.

SECTION 6. The throw-in starts when the ball is at the disposal of a player entitled to the throw-in and he shall pass the ball directly into the court so that, after it crosses the boundary line and before going out of bounds, it touches or is touched by another player on the court within 5 seconds from the time the throw-in starts. Until the passed ball has crossed the plane of the boundary: (a) the thrower shall not leave the designated throw-in spot; (b) no player shall have any part of his person over the boundary line; and (c) teammates shall not occupy adjacent positions near the boundary if an opponent desires one of the positions. The 3-foot restraining line is sometimes the temporary boundary as in rule 1-2.

> Question.—B has the ball out of bounds. His throw-in: (a) enters a basket before touching anyone; or (b) strikes ring or backboard and rebounds; or (c) touches another player and then enters basket. Ans.—(a) Violation by B. A's ball at either end of the nearer free throw line extended. No goal because ball is dead. (b) Ball becomes alive when touched. (c)—Legal goal for team in whose basket the ball remains or through which it passes.

Rule 8   Free Throw

SECTION 1. When a free throw is awarded, an official shall take the ball to the free throw line of the offended team. After allowing reasonable time for players to take their positions, he shall put the ball in play by placing it at the disposal of the free thrower. The same procedure shall be followed for each free throw of a multiple throw. During a free throw for personal foul, each of the lane spaces adjacent to the end line shall be occupied by one opponent of the free thrower. A teammate of the free thrower is entitled to the next adjacent lane space on each side and to each other alternate position along each lane line. Not more than one player may occupy any part of the first, second or third lane spaces. If the ball is to become dead when the last free throw for a specific penalty is not successful, players shall not take positions along the free throw lane.

NOTE—To avoid disconcerting the free thrower, neither official should stand in the free throw lane or the lane extended.

SECTION 2. The free throw or throws awarded because of a personal foul shall be attempted by the offended player. If such player must withdraw because of an injury or disqualification, his substitute shall attempt the throw or throws unless no substitute is available, in which event any teammate may attempt the throw or throws.

SECTION 3. The free throw awarded because of a technical foul may be attempted by any player, including an entering substitute, of the offended team.

SECTION 4. The try for goal shall be made within 10 seconds after the ball has been placed at the disposal of the free thrower at the free throw line. This shall apply to each free throw.

SECTION 5. After a free throw which is not followed by another free throw, the ball shall be put in play by a throw-in: (a) as after a field goal (7-5) if the try is for a personal foul and is successful; or (b) by any player of the free thrower's team from out of bounds at mid-court if the free throw is for a technical foul.

SECTION 6. If a free throw for a personal foul is unsuccessful, or if there is a multiple throw for a personal foul (or fouls) and the last free throw is unsuccessful, the ball remains alive.

If there is a multiple throw and both a personal and technical foul are involved, the tries shall be attempted in the order in which the related fouls were called and if the last try is for a technical foul the ball shall be put in play as after any technical foul.

SECTION 7. After the last free throw following a false double foul (4-8(b)), the ball shall be put in play by a jump at center between any two opponents.

Ques.—Two free throws are awarded to A and before time is in, one free throw is awarded to B. What is the correct procedure? Ans.—Jump ball at center after the third free throw.

Rule 9   Violations and Penalties

A player shall not—

SECTION 1. Violate the free throw provisions: (a) The try shall be attempted from within the free throw circle and behind the free throw line. (b) After the ball is placed at the disposal of a free thrower: (1) he shall throw within 10 seconds and in such a way that the ball enters the basket or touches the ring before the free throw ends; (2) no opponent may disconcert the free thrower; and (3) the free thrower shall not have either foot beyond the vertical plane of that edge of the free throw line which is farther from the basket; and no other player of either team shall have either foot beyond the vertical plane or cylinder of the outside edge of any lane boundary, nor beyond the vertical plane of any edge of the space (2 inches by 36 inches) designated by a lane space mark or the space (12 inches by 36 inches) designated by a neutral zone mark, nor enter nor leave the lane space which is nearest the end line. The restrictions in (3) apply until the ball touches the ring or backboard or until the free throw ends. (c) An opponent of the free thrower shall occupy each lane space adjacent to the end line during the try, and no teammate of the free thrower may occupy either of these lane spaces.

PENALTY—(1) If violation is by the free thrower or his teammate only, no point can be scored by that throw. Ball becomes dead when violation occurs. Ball is awarded out of bounds on the sideline to the free thrower's team opposite center circle after a technical foul, and to any opponent out of bounds at either end of the free throw line extended after a personal foul. (2) If violation is by the free thrower's opponent only: if the try is successful, the goal counts and violation is disregarded; if it is not successful, a substitute throw shall be attempted by the same thrower under conditions the same as for the throw for which it is substituted. In these cases, ball becomes dead when the free throw ends. (3) If there is a violation by each team, ball becomes dead when violation by the free thrower's team occurs, no point can be scored, and play shall be resumed by a jump between any two opponents in the nearest circle. The out of bounds provision in penalty item (1) and the jump ball provision in penalty item (3) do not apply if the free throw is to be followed by another free throw, or if there are free throws by both teams. In penalty item (3), if an opponent of the thrower touches the free throw before it has touched the ring, the violation for failure to touch the ring is ignored.

Ques.—During a free throw by A1, B1 pushes A2 and also B1 or B2 is in the lane too soon. Ans.—If the free throw is not successful, award a substitute free throw and also penalize the foul.

SECTION 2. Cause the ball to go out of bounds.

Ques.—Dribbler in control steps on or outside a boundary, but does not touch the ball while he is out of bounds. Is this a violation? Ans.—Yes.

SECTION 3. Violate provisions governing the throw-in. The thrower-in shall not: (a) leave the designated throw-in spot; (b) fail to pass the ball directly into the court so that after it crosses the boundary line it touches or is touched by another player on the court before going out of bounds; (c) consume more than 5 seconds from the time the throw-in starts until it touches or is touched by a player on the court; (d) carry the ball onto the court; (e) touch it in the court before it has touched another player; nor (f) throw the ball so that it enters a basket before touching anyone.

No player shall: (g) have any part of his person over the boundary line before the ball has been passed across the line; nor (h) become the thrower-in after an official has designated another player.

Ques.—On throw-in, A steps on the line or reaches through its plane while holding the ball. Ans.—Violation. Allowance should be made if space is limited.

SECTION 4. Run with the ball, kick it, strike it with the fist or cause it to enter and pass through the basket from below.

NOTE—Kicking the ball is a violation only when it is a positive act; accidentally striking the ball with the foot or leg is not a violation.

Ques.—What is kicking the ball? Ans.—Kicking the ball is striking it intentionally with the knee or any part of the leg or foot below the knee. It is a fundamental of basketball that the ball must be played with the hands.

SECTION 5. Dribble a second time after his first dribble has ended, unless it is after he has lost control because of: (a) a try for field goal after the ball is in flight; or (b) a bat by an opponent; or (c) a pass or fumble which has then touched another player. He shall not make more than one air dribble during a dribble.

SECTION 6. Violate any provision of 6-4. If both teams simultaneously commit violations during the jump ball, or if the official makes a bad toss, the toss should be repeated.

SECTION 7. Remain for more than 3 seconds in that part of his free throw lane between the end line and the farther edge of the free throw line while the ball is in control of his team. Allowance shall be made for a player who, having been in the restricted area for less than 3 seconds, dribbles in to try for goal.

Ques.—Does the 3-second restriction apply: (a) to a player who has only one foot touching the lane boundary; or (b) while the ball is dead or is in flight on a try? Ans.—(a) Yes, the line is part of the lane. (b) No, the team is not in control.

SECTION 8. Be (and his team shall not be) in continuous control of a ball which is in his back court for more than 10 consecutive seconds.

SECTION 9. Be the first to touch a ball which he or a teammate caused to go from front court to back court by being the last to touch the ball while it was in control of his team and before it went to the back court. EXCEPTION: This restriction does not apply if, after a jump ball in the center circle, the player who first secures control of the tapped ball is in his front court at the time he secures such control and he causes the ball to go to his back court not later than the first loss of player control by him and provided it is the first time the ball is in his back court following the jump ball.

Ques.—A receives pass in his front court and throws ball to his back court where ball: (a) is touched by a teammate; or (b) goes directly out of bounds; or (c) lies or bounces with all players hesitating to touch it. Ans.—Violation when touched in (a). In (b) it is a violation for going out of bounds. In (c) ball is alive so that B may secure control. If A touches ball first, it is a violation. The ball continues to be in team control of A and if A does not touch it the 10-second count starts when the ball arrives in the back court.

SECTION 10. Excessively swing his arms or elbows, even though there is no contact with an opponent.

PENALTY—(Sections 2 to 10): Ball becomes dead or remains dead when violation occurs. Ball is awarded to a nearby opponent for a throw-in at the out of bounds spot nearest the violation. If the ball passes through a basket during the dead ball period immediately following a violation, no point can be scored and the ball is awarded to an opponent out of bounds at either end of that free throw line extended nearer the goal through which the ball was thrown.

SECTION 11. (a) Touch the ball or basket when the ball is on or within either basket; nor touch the ball when it: (b) is touching the cylinder having the ring as its lower base; or (c) is not touching the cylinder but is in downward flight during a try for field goal while the entire ball is above the basket ring level and before the ball has touched the ring or the try has ended. Exception: In (a) or (b), if a player near his own basket has his hand legally in contact with the ball, it is not a violation if his contact with the ball continues after it enters the cylinder, or if, in such action, he touches the basket.

PENALTY—If violation is at the opponent's basket, offended team is awarded one point if during a free throw and two points in any other case. The crediting of the score and subsequent procedure is the same as if the awarded score had resulted from the ball having gone through the basket, except that the official shall hand the ball to a player of the team entitled to the throw-in.

If violation is at a team's own basket, no points can be scored and the ball is awarded to the offended team at the out of bounds spot on the side at either end of the free throw line extended.

If there is a violation by both teams, play shall be resumed by a jump ball between any two opponents in the nearest circle.

Ques.—While the ball is in flight on a try for field goal by A, a teammate of A pushes an opponent. After this personal foul, the ball is on the ring when B bats it away. Which infraction should be penalized? Ans.—Both. Award 2 points to A. Then penalize for personal foul.

Rule 10 Fouls and Penalties

A. TECHNICAL FOUL . . .

A team shall not—

SECTION 1. Delay the game by preventing ball from being promptly made alive, or by allowing the game to develop into an actionless contest.

This includes the following and similar acts:

(a) When clock is not running—consuming a full minute through not being ready when it is time to start either half; or

(b) Failure to supply scorers with data as outlined in rule 3-2; or

(c) When behind in the score or while on defense with the score tied and after a warning by an official, failing to be reasonably active in attempts to secure the ball if on defense or to advance the ball beyond the mid-court area if on offense and there is no opposing action in the mid-court area.

SECTION 2. Be charged with an excess time-out (5-11).

SECTION 3. Have more than five squad members participating simultaneously.

A player shall not—

SECTION 4. (a) **Participate after changing his number** without reporting it to the scorers and an official;

(b) **Participate after having been disqualified;**

(c) **Attempt to gain an advantage:** by interfering with ball after a goal or by failing to immediately pass ball to nearer official if in control when a violation is called, or by repeated infractions of 9-3g and h;

(d) **Wear an illegal number;**

(e) **Grasp the basket;**

(f) **Leave the court** for an unauthorized reason; or

(g) **Purposely delay his return** to the court after being legally out of bounds.

> **Ques.**—A player steps out of bounds to avoid contact. **Ans.**—This is not a foul unless he leaves to conceal himself or to deceive in some other way. If he is a dribbler, ball is out of bounds.

SECTION 5. Use unsportsmanlike tactics, such as: (a) disrespectfully addressing or contacting an official, or failing to raise his hand at arm's length above his head after being charged with a foul or raising it in such a way as to indicate resentment; (b) using profanity; (c) baiting an opponent or obstructing his vision by waving hands near his eyes; (d) climbing on a teammate to secure greater height to handle ball; (e) knowingly attempting a free throw to which he was not entitled; or (f) causing unsportsmanlike contact as in 4-8 (i).

NOTE—Contact after the ball has become dead is ignored unless it is unsportsmanlike or is during a throw-in.

A substitute shall not—

SECTION 6. **Enter the court:** (a) without reporting to scorers; or (b) without his name appearing on the pregame squad list; or (c) (unless between halves) without being beckoned by an official.

A coach, substitute, team attendant or follower shall not—

SECTION 7. **Disrespectfully address** an official nor attempt to influence his decisions; nor disrespectfully address or bait an opponent; nor indicate his objection to an official's decision by rising from the bench or using gestures; nor do anything to incite undesirable crowd reactions; nor shall he enter the court unless by permission of an official to attend an injured player. Coaches shall remain seated on the bench except, while the clock is stopped, they may leave the bench to direct or encourage players who are on the court. Coaches may, at any time, leave the bench to confer with substitutes, to signal players to request a time-out, or to perform other necessary coaching responsibilities. During an intermission or a time-out charged to a team, the coach and/or team attendants may confer with their players at or near their bench.

PENALTY—(Sections 1 to 7): Offended team is awarded one free throw and its captain shall designate the thrower. A second free throw shall be awarded if the foul is flagrant. EXCEPTION: If more than one infraction by the same team is involved in section 1(a) or 4(d), or if two or more teammates are involved in sections 3 or 6, only one free throw is awarded.

For sections 3 and 4 (a) or (b), an infraction shall be penalized if it is discovered during the time the rule is being violated or an error for failure to penalize may be corrected by applying rule 2-10.

For sections 4(a) and (b), or for flagrant or persistent infraction of any section, the offender shall be disqualified. If the offender is a coach, substitute, team attendant or follower, he shall be banished from the vicinity of the court. For failure to comply, referee may forfeit the game.

B. PERSONAL FOUL . . .

SECTION 8. A player shall not: hold, push, charge, trip; nor impede the progress of an opponent by extended arm, shoulder, hip or knee, or by bending the body into other than a normal position; nor use any rough tactics. He shall not contact an opponent with his hand unless such contact is only with the opponent's hand while it is on the ball and is incidental to an attempt to play the ball. Contact caused by a defensive player approaching the ball holder from behind is a form of pushing and that caused by the momentum of a player who has thrown for goal is a form of charging.

A dribbler shall not charge into nor contact an opponent in his path nor attempt to dribble between two opponents or between an opponent and a boundary, unless the space is such as to provide a reasonable chance for him to go through without contact. If a dribbler, without contact, passes an opponent sufficiently to have head and shoulders in advance of him, the greater responsibility for subsequent contact is on the opponent. If a dribbler in his progress has established a straight line path, he may not be crowded out of that path but, if an opponent is able legally to establish a defensive position in that path, the dribbler must avoid contact by changing direction or ending his dribble.

A player who screens shall not: (a) when he is behind a stationary opponent, take a position closer than a normal step from him; (b) when he assumes a position at the side or in front of a stationary opponent, make contact with him; (c) take a position so close to a moving opponent that this opponent cannot avoid contact by stopping or changing direction. In (c), the speed of the player to be screened will determine where the screener may take his stationary position. This position will vary and may be one to two normal steps or strides from his opponent. (d) Move after assuming his screening position, except in the same direction and path of his opponent.

If the screener violates any of these provisions and contact results, he has committed a personal foul.

PENALTY—Offender is charged with one foul and if it is his fifth personal foul, or if it is flagrant, he is disqualified. (1) Offended player (or his substitute, if such player is disqualified or injured) is awarded one free throw unless it is a double foul or a player control foul. (2) Unless it is a multiple foul, a second free throw is awarded if the foul: (a) is flagrant or intentional, including one by a player who does not make reasonable effort to avoid contact and who tries to reach the ball from an unfavorable position: or (b) is committed against a field goal thrower whose try is not successful; or (c) is a common foul (except as noted in (1) above) which occurs after the offending team has been charged during the half with four personal fouls in a game played in quarters or with six personal fouls in a game played in halves, and provided the first free throw for the common foul is successful. (Extra periods are an extension of the 2nd half.)

NOTE—If there is any doubt as to whether there is player control during the time he or a teammate commits a common foul, the interpretation shall be that the ball was in player control.

Ques. (1)—A guard moves into the path of a dribbler and contact occurs. Who is responsible? Ans.—Either may be responsible but the greater responsibility is that of the guard if the guard conforms to the following principles which officials use in reaching a decision. The guard is assumed to have established a guarding position if he is in the dribbler's path facing him. No specific stance or distance is specified. It is assumed the guard may shift to maintain his position in the path of the dribbler provided he does not charge into the dribbler nor otherwise cause contact as outlined in the 2nd paragraph of 10-8. However, if he jumps into position, both feet must return to the floor after the jump, before he has established guarding position.

The responsibility of the dribbler for contact is not shifted merely because the guard turns or ducks to absorb shock when contact caused by the dribbler is imminent. The guard may not cause contact by moving under or in front of a passer or thrower after he is in the air with feet off the floor.

Ques. (2)—One or both fouls of either a multiple foul or of a double foul is flagrant. What is the procedure? **Ans.**—For a multiple foul, one free throw is awarded for each foul. For a double foul no free throws are awarded. In either case, any player who commits a flagrant foul is disqualified.

Ques. (3)—Does goal count if ball goes in the basket after a foul? **Ans.**—Yes, unless ball becomes dead (as in rule 6-7) before it enters the basket.

OFFICIAL BASKETBALL SIGNALS

For free throw violation:
Use Signals 2 and 18

For basket interference:
Use Signals 11 or 12 and 13

INDEX

796.32
G

Garstang, James

AUTHOR

Basketball the modern way

TITLE

796.32
G   Garstang, James
        Basketball the modern way

947

947

DATE DUE

GAYLORD   PERRY   PRINTED IN U.S A.